THE
MAKING OF AMERICA
SERIES

HIGHLANDS
NEW JERSEY

Ann McNeil (1896–1998), poet and life resident of Highlands, wrote the following of Highlands: "Our town is small / Just one mile square / But it is rumored / That if you dare / Allow its beach sand / In your shoes / You'll fall beneath / its spell forever."

Cover: This historic c. 1910 view looks across the Shrewsbury River from Sandy Hook.

THE
MAKING OF AMERICA
SERIES

HIGHLANDS
NEW JERSEY

JOHN P. KING

ARCADIA

Published by Arcadia Publishing,
an imprint of Tempus Publishing, Inc.
2 Cumberland Street
Charleston, SC 29401

Printed in Great Britain.

Library of Congress Catalog Card Number: 2001091210

For all general information contact Arcadia Publishing at:
Telephone 843-853-2070
Fax 843-853-0044
E-Mail sales@arcadiapublishing.com

For customer service and orders:
Toll-Free 1-888-313-2665

Visit us on the Internet at http://www.arcadiapublishing.com

Patterson and Parker children are shown here in the heart of Parkertown in 1919. From left to right, they are as follows: Michael O. Patterson, Joe Patterson, Bill Patterson (on hood), Harriet Parker, Dave Patterson, Catherine Parker, Eddie Patterson, Flora Parker, Stewart Patterson, Tillie Parker, Midge Patterson, and Annie Patterson.

CONTENTS

This book is dedicated to the

Bahrs family of Highlands

and in particular to

John "Buddy" Bahrs,

who loved Highlands, its people, and its rich history.

John "Buddy" A. Bahrs (1908–1998) served as Highlands mayor from 1965 to 1968.

INTRODUCTION

Highlands, a town defined by its rugged high hills and embraced by the surrounding waters of the ocean, bay, and river, has always been both a desirable destination for thousands of visitors and a comfortable home for some 1,200 families. Today, visitors know the little (just .67 square mile) town for its many fine seafood restaurants located right on the river, its marinas, its fast and comfortable commuter ferries to Manhattan, its historic Twin Lights, and its being the gateway to Sandy Hook National Recreation Area, all with a wonderful, quaint character and seaside feel.

Years ago, from as early as the 1830s through the 1960s, city people knew Highlands as a summer resort, a haven from the heat and hard life in the cities. They would come for a week, a month, or the whole summer to stay first in tents and later in bungalows, boarding houses, and hotels. Thousands used to come to spend the day, arriving on trains and steamboats and later in family-packed automobiles, breathing in deeply the clean salt air, eating locally caught seafood—especially the clams, for which Highlands for many generations has had an enviable reputation—enjoying the sun and water on the beaches.

Highlands has been the scene of many exciting and historically significant happenings. The explorers Verrazzano and Hudson made the first European contact with the Lenape Indians, who were native to the Highlands area, changing their world forever. During the American Revolution, enemy forces executed national patriot and local hero Captain Joshua Huddy in Highlands, causing excited debate in the capitals of the world. Marconi, the father of radio, came to Highlands Twin Lights hill to excite the world with the wonder of wireless radio communication. Gertrude Ederle, who summered with her family in Highlands and learned to swim in its Shrewsbury River, excited all America, cheering her as America's Best Girl, the first American and the first woman to swim the English Channel in world-record time. Discovery of gold coins on a river beach caused an excitement of Gold Rush fever as thousands of get-rich-quick prospectors ripped through the Highlands sands.

In the year 2000, there was an excitement in Highlands once again, then in its Centennial Celebration of 100 years as a Borough, as the town looked forward to a new year, a new century, a new millennium of continued progress. Highlands was and is still today a *hometown*. From its waterfront neighborhoods, to its active restaurant and business area, to its homes in the spectacular Highlands hills, this little community, proud of its exciting history, is equally proud of being a good family town.

7

1. The First Europeans Arrive

The early sixteenth and seventeenth centuries are times of accidental discovery and tentative exploration of the Highlands by French, Italian, Spanish, English, and Dutch navigators, attracted by the prominence of the "High Lands." They came and stayed just long enough to deem the area worthy of a later return in force. The native Lenape always remembered how they met them, how remarkable it all was, and how badly mistaken they had been to think it was their Manito coming to them.

In June 1524, Giovanni da Verrazzano, an Italian from Florence, was sailing the *Dauphine* on a voyage of exploration for King Francis I of France. In his report, he wrote that he found a "very agreeable place between two small but prominent hills," the Highlands and Staten Island hills between which "a very wide river, deep at its mouth [the Hudson River], flowed out into the sea." Verrazzano guided his ship around the tip of Sandy Hook, and as he sailed in, he viewed the green oak–topped Highlands hills. He explored within Sandy Hook bay and came closer to the hills, anchoring probably within the Horse Shoe Cove, well sheltered from storms.

Verrazzano, with modern political correctness, paid a compliment to one of the noble supporters of his royal benefactor, Francis I, and named after him the hill where the Twin Lights are located today. At this time, the Hook was attached to the northeastern part of the Highlands mainland, and the ocean broke right at the base of the hill, the barrier beach of Sea Bright not yet existing. Verrazzano noted, "We baptized a little mountain by the sea 'Di San Paolo' (*of St. Paul*) after the Count."

With his crew, Verrazzano continued exploring the area that centuries later thousands upon thousands of visitors would know and love as Highlands, even meeting and describing for the King the native American Indian residents. The voyagers went onto the land, which they found densely populated. Verrazzano described the Lenape as dressed in bird feathers of various colors, coming toward the landing party, and he assumed, joyfully, "uttering loud cries of wonderment and showing the safest place to beach the boat."

Suddenly, a "violent, unfavorable wind blew in from the sea," perhaps a northeast storm, or nor'easter, so common to the Highlands area, forcing the crew to return to the *Dauphine* and set sail to the open sea. They left "this land with much regret on account of its favorable conditions and beauty." By July 1524, Verrazzano, the leader of the first Europeans to leave their footprints in the Highlands hills, was back in Dieppe, France, spreading word of the marvelous sights he had seen.

Lenape tribespeople in the Highlands are watching in wonder and awe at the coming of the Half Moon *into Sandy Hook Bay.*

Another navigator was preparing a voyage of exploration for a passage to the Indies for Charles V of Spain. By May 1525, the Portuguese Estevan Gomez viewed the Highlands and the Hook. Unfortunately, he left no report of his experiences, but today's researchers and historians know from the Diego Ribero chart of 1529 (found in the Vatican Museums in Rome) what lands he saw.

On the map, Sandy Hook is clearly visible and is so named for the first time in history, "Cabo de Arenas," or "Cape of Sand." The Navesink and Shrewsbury Rivers are seen flowing directly out to the ocean, with traces of the barrier beach forming in lower Sea Bright, and they are labeled "Rio de Santiago," or "River of St. James."

Nearly a century passed before another European came to view the Highlands, while in search of a passage to Asia. In 1609, a company of wealthy Amsterdam merchants bought a ship called the *Half Moon* and chose the Englishman Henry Hudson, an able and very experienced master, to form a crew and outfit the ship for a voyage of exploration into the West.

Fortunately for Hudson, the Highlands, and history, he brought aboard an officer of keen ability at sea and of capable literary skill: Robert Juet of Lime-House. Juet wrote a detailed account of this trip called *Third Voyage of Master Henrie Hudson.*

Having sailed down from New England, Hudson reversed course off Virginia and sailed north searching the coastline for likely water passages through the land mass and barrier of North America to Asia. After testing Chesapeake Bay and then Delaware Bay and finding them fruitless, he sailed off past Barnegat Bay until on September 2, 1609, he anchored the *Half Moon* in 8 fathoms of water at five o'clock. Hudson took sightings of the coastline, which he plotted at 8 degrees from North, and then he saw them, the

American Indians and Europeans encountered each other close-up as Hudson's Half Moon *moved up the river above Manhattan, just as the Lenape and Hudson's men had met for the first time in Highlands.*

Highlands. Juet recorded in his diary, "For to the Northward off us we saw high hils. For the day before we found not above two degrees of Variation," followed by the words so frequently quoted, "This is a very good Land to fall with, and a pleasant Land to see." The next morning on September 3, a southeast breeze appeared to have cleared away the mist, and as Hudson moved his ship farther north for a better look, Juet wrote that the "Land is very pleasant and high and bold to fall withall."

Emotions similar to Juet's expressions of awe, with perhaps a bit more enthusiasm, at the magnificent views of the Highlands, have been repeated again and again since Juet's first words, at different times, under different circumstances, in different words and languages, whenever seen by one coming upon the Highlands for the first time.

One can let Juet speak for himself in his old fashioned words as the *Half Moon* came into Sandy Hook Bay, which was just teeming with fish, reminding one of the Lenape word for the area, "Navesink," or "Place of Good Fishing":

> So wee went in to our Boate to sound and found no lesse water than foure, five, sixe, and seven fathoms and returned in an Houre and a Halfe. So wee weighed and went in and rode in five fathoms, Ozie ground, and saw many Salmons, and Mullets, and Rayes very great. The height is 40 degrees 30 minutes. [*i.e.* latitude].
>
> The fourth [September 4] in the morning as soone as the day was light wee saw that it was good riding farther up. So wee sent our Boate to sound and found

> that it was a very good Harbour, and foure and five fathoms two Cables length
> from the Shoare. Then we weighed and went in with our ship. Then our Boate
> went on Land with our Net to fish and caught ten great Mullets of a foot and a
> halfe long a peece and a Ray as great as foure men could hale into the ship.

Having experienced Horse Shoe Cove and its bounty of big fish, Hudson's party was forced to encounter the local people, the Lenape Indians. Juet noted the following:

> This day the people of the country came aboard of us, seeming very glad of our
> coming and brought greene Tobacco and gave us of it for Knives and Beads.
> They goe in Deere skins loose, well dressed (*i.e.* tanned). They have yellow
> Copper. They desire Cloathes and are very Civill. They have great store of Maiz
> or Indian Wheate whereof they make good Bread. The country is full of great
> and tall Oakes.

The crew was sent by boat to the Highlands mainland where there apparently was a Lenape village. Juet recorded his impression of the village as follows:

> Our men went on Land there and saw a great store of Men, Women, and
> Children who gave them Tobacco at their coming on Land.

Hudson and his men were the second and better documented Europeans to set foot on the Highlands sands, and the first to climb into the hills and admire the fantastic vista across the bay and ocean. Juet recalled the experience as follows:

> So they went up into the Woods and saw a great store of goodly Oakes and some
> Currents. For one of them came aboard and brought some dryed and gave me
> some which were sweet and good.
>   This day many of the people came aboard, some in Mantles of Feathers and
> some in Skinnes of divers sorts of good Furres. Some women also came to us
> with Hempe. They had red Copper Tobacco pipes and other things of Copper
> they did weare about their neckes. At night they went on Land againe, so wee
> rode very quiet, but durst not trust them.

Their distrust of the Indians is without reason at this point in Juet's narrative and was possibly included here if this and the next section were composed together. Now in secure anchorage close to the Highlands shore, perhaps in the deepwater off Gravelly Point, Hudson began exploring the area west of the Hook up to the Raritan, Newark Bay, the Kill Van Kull, and the Narrows. Then something went terribly wrong late that afternoon, described as follows:

> Our Master sent John Coleman with foure men in our Boate over to the North-
> side. . . . They were set upon by two Canoes, the one having twelve, the other
> fourteen men. The night came on and it began to Rayne so that their Match

went out. And they also had one man slain in the fight, which was an Englishman, named John Coleman, with an Arrow shot into his throat, and two men hurt. The seventh was faire and by ten of the Clocke they returned aboard the ship and brought our dead man with them, whom we carried on Land and buryed and named the point after his name, Colmans Point.

John Coleman is remembered in history as the first European to die in the New World of America. The exact location of his grave is in dispute, although it may have been on Sandy Hook rather than on the bayshore coast, where the burial party would have feared encountering more Lenape.

Hudson's men expected a full-scale attack and were suspicious of the Lenape friendliness. They raised the wooden sides on their boat as a protection from arrows and kept a careful watch all night long. The next day, the eighth, some Lenape natives approached and again came aboard the *Half Moon* with tobacco and maize to trade for knives and beads. The crew was uneasy and mystified that the Indians offered no hostility and made no show of remorse for the death of John Coleman. Their crew's anxieties increased the next day as seen with the following:

> The ninth, faire weather. In the morning, two great Canoes came aboard full of men; the one with their Bowes and Arrows and the other in shew of buying Knives, to betray us; but wee perceived of their intent. We took two of them to have kept them and put red Coates on them and would not suffer the others to come neere us. So they went on Land and two others came aboard in a Canoe. Wee tooke the one and let the other goe; but hee which wee had taken, got up and leapt over board.

At this point of deteriorated relations with the Lenape, Hudson left the Highlands area immediately and the next day set about exploration of the river that bears his name, having gone as far as Albany before abandoning the search for the elusive passage to the riches of the East. Then Juet concludes his journal with Henry Hudson's last look upon the Highlands,

> The fourth [October 4] . . . We . . . steered away . . . into the mayne sea and the Land on the Souther-side of the Bay or Inlet did beare at noone West and South foure Leagues from us.

The Lenape did not possess a written language and depended upon oral tradition to preserve the records of events, passing down to each generation stories like "The Coming of the White Man," which ultimately was written down for them in 1819 by John Heckewelder, a missionary to the Lenape. The events recorded here generally are accepted as the arrival of Henry Hudson and the *Half Moon* in September 1609:

> A long time ago before men with a white skin had ever been seen, some Indians fishing at a place where the sea widens, espied something at a distance moving

This historically accurate replica of Henry Hudson's Half Moon *sailed on a voyage of the "rediscovery of Highlands" on September 16, 1993, recreating the journey by Hudson and his men in 1609.*

upon the water. They hurried ashore, collected their neighbors and together returned and viewed intently this astonishing phenomenon.

What it could be baffled conjecture. Some supposed it to be a large fish or other animal; others that it was a large house floating upon the sea.

Perceiving it moving toward the land, the spectators concluded that it would be proper to send runners in different directions to carry the news to their scattered chiefs, that they might send off for the immediate attendance of their warriors.

They arrived in numbers to behold the sight and perceiving that it was actually moving toward them, that it was coming into the bay, they conjectured that it must be a remarkably large house in which the Manito or Great Spirit was coming to visit them. They were much afraid, yet under no apprehension that the Great Spirit would injure them.

The chiefs now assembled at New York Island and consulted in what manner they should receive their Manito. Meat was prepared for a sacrifice. . . .

Utterly at a loss as to what to do and distracted alternately between hope and fear, in the confusion a great dance was begun.

In the meantime fresh runners arrived, declaring it to be a great house of various colors and full of living creatures. Others declared it positively full of people of different color and dress from them and that one appeared altogether in red. This then must be the Manito. They were lost in admiration, could not imagine what the vessel was, or what all this portended for them.

They were now hailed in a language they could not understand. They answered by a shout or yell in their own way. The house stopped. A small canoe came on shore with the red man in it. The chief and wise men formed a circle into which the red man and two attendants entered. He saluted them with a friendly countenance and they returned the salute after their own manner.

They were amazed at their color and their dress, especially at him. They thought that he must be a great Manito but wondered why he should have a white skin. And they wondered what all this portended for the Lenape.

From the historic first encounter between the Lenape in New Jersey and the Europeans to the 1802 removal of 100 remaining Lenape Indians to lands in New York was a long period of hardships for the tribe. They suffered losses to their ancestral ways of life and an incredible decrease in their numbers, through war, disease, and alcohol abuse. Today, little remains to attest to the Lenape presence—just museum artifacts and place names of Indian origin.

2. THE PRE-COLONIAL PERIOD

About the middle of the seventeenth century, both Dutch and English in New Holland looked out across the lower bay toward the High Lands of the Navesink and saw them as a prominent mark of land guiding Dutch traders with the Lenape there and later English settlers on the Lenape lands. Richard Hartshorne bought their land and settled it, for it was a pleasant region to see and live upon, in a manner common for Europeans and extraordinary for Indians who, just 150 years after first encountering men with white skin on their lands, were compelled to leave it forever.

The Lenape Indians of the Navesink area maintained year-round settlements rather than seasonal summer villages in the hills that make up the Highlands of today. The archaeology at Oyster Point in Red Bank and historical references indicate year-round and permanent inhabitation.

Settlement by Europeans, in permanent structures, such as homes, hotels, taverns, and churches, intended for constant inhabitation, first took place in 1678, when the Englishman Richard Hartshorne built his home, "Portland," on the Navesink River at the "Cove." From 1609, when Henry Hudson sailed his *Half Moon* in Sandy Hook Bay and his Dutch crew first set foot in the Highlands, to 1664, when the British took control of the area, the Dutch were unable to establish any settlement in the Highlands.

The Dutch explorer and mapmaker Adriaen Block charted the area and made it easier for Dutch traders to follow after 1613, but they did not settle. When the British challenged their presence in 1634, the Dutch government officially denied having made any settlement in the area, while admitting that the Dutch West India Company was trading with Lenape in huts in Bergen and Hoboken.

In 1663, when the British and Dutch vigorously tried to outmaneuver each other in gaining a foothold in the Highlands, British from Gravesend on Long Island came across to the Highlands looking to buy land from the Lenape, thus implying that no Dutch had already bought land from the Indians and begun settlement. A Dutch report in that same year states that the Navesink area is "a place where no Christians are residing, but only wild barbarians."

After a confrontation in Highlands just north of the present bridge between a party led by Cortelyou from New Amsterdam and a band of British from Long Island, the Dutch ordered that a fort be built to hold the area. They reported that "the English from

Gravesend and some other vagabonds intend to go to the Newesinghs in the spring and take possession of the land there." The fort was never built.

In the spring, James Hubbard, John Bowne, and William Goulding purchased the lands of the Highlands from the Lenape. Later in the summer, Peter Stuyvesant surrendered all of New Netherlands to British Deputy Governor Richard Nichols.

The Highlands was now ready for British settlement. In 1665, Nichols issued the famous Monmouth Patent, which allotted the Highlands area to William Goulding. Richard Hartshorne, who had come from England in 1669, purchased vast tracts of land in Middletown in the Keansburg area, and in late 1672, he bought Goulding's rights to the Highlands. After the Monmouth Patent was declared void, Hartshorne, in December 1678, received 500 acres on the Highlands peninsula as compensation for his loss. The next year he built his home, "Portland," in the Highlands along the Navesink River south of Clay Pit Creek.

Settlement actually within the borough borders in Highlands is recorded on a British Museum figurative map of 1682. It clearly shows Hartshorne's home at "Portland" and a house located on the hill below today's Twin Lights. On this same map, one can count about 30 houses in the Middletown area from the village (where 36 lots were laid out December 30, 1667) down to the bay; in Shrewsbury, 10 houses; Highlands, only 2; and in the location of Atlantic Highlands, only 1 house. The numbers may indicate only larger-sized communities, although written reports of the time suggest at least three to four houses at Portland Poynte or Atlantic Highlands (where ten lots had been laid out on December 15, 1667), which served as a governmental seat along with Shrewsbury and Middletown during this early period. Whatever the number of settlers' homes in the Highlands at this time in the last two decades of the seventeenth century, the Lenape continued to have and to exert a presence here, especially to Richard Hartshorne.

Richard Hartshorne left England for New Jersey in 1669, and being one of the most successful and most literate landholders, he was asked by the proprietary promoters of New Jersey to write a piece to encourage others like him to follow after him and purchase Jersey lands upon which to settle. His contribution set in the form of a letter to a friend did a wonderful job not only as propaganda, but as a historically useful description of early life. In his piece, one should note how beneficial the Lenape were to Hartshorne and the first settlers and consider this in relation to the situation of just a few years later. Hartshorne wrote the following:

> Dear Friend: My love is to thee and to thy wife. . . . Now I shall give some information concerning New Jersie. Thee desireth to know how I live. Through the goodness of the Lord I live very well, keeping between 30 and 40 head of cows, and 7 or 8 horses to ride upon. There are several towns settled in this Province, viz., Shrewsbury, Middletown . . . Piscattaway, Woodbridge, Elizabethtown, New Coake, and Bergen. Most of these Towns have about 100 families; and the least 40. The country is very beautiful. In Middletown where I live, in 6 years and upwards there have died but one woman about 80 years old, one man about 60, and a boy about 5 years, and one little infant or 2. There are

This aerial view shows the relationship of Highlands to Sandy Hook and New York, some 25 miles in the distance, and the interconnecting river, bay, and ocean.

in this Town in twenty-five families about 95 children, most of them under 12 years of age and all lusty children.

The produce of this Provence is chiefly Wheat, Barley, Oates, Beans, Beef, Pork, Pease, Tobacco, Indian corn, butter, cheese, hemp and flax, French beans, Strawberries, Carrots, Parsnips, Cabbidge, Turnips, Radishes, Onions, Cucumbers, Water-mellons, Squashes; also our soil is verry fertile for Apples, Pears, Plums, Quinces, Currans red and white, Gooseberries, Cherries, and Peaches in abundance.

The Country is greatly supplied with Creeks and Rivers which afford stores of Fish, Perch, Roach, Baste, Sheepsheads, Oysters, Crabs, Sturgeons, Eels. . . . You may buy as much Fish of an Indian for half a pound of Powder as will serve 6 or 8 men.

Deer are also very plenty in this Province. We can buy a fat Buck of the Indians . . . for a pound and a half of Powder or Lead or any other trade equivalent . . . Our Beef and Pork are verry fat and good. . . . We make English Bread and Beer; besides we have several sorts of other Drink.

In traveling in the Country and coming to any House, they generally ask you to eat and drink and take Tobacco . . .

Here are abundance of Chestnuts, Walnuts, Mulberries, and Grapes red and white; our Horses and Mares run in the open Woods and we give them no meal Winter nor Summer, unless we work them; but our cows must be looked after.

Our Timber Stands for fences about the Land we manure. We plough our land with Oxen. . . . A man that has three or four sonns or servants that can work along with him will down with Timber and get corn quickly.

> The best coming to this country is at the Spring or Fall. . . . In the Winter we make good fires and we eat good Meat and our women and children are healthy. . . . One great happiness we enjoy, which is we are very quiet. . . .
>
> This is a rare place for any poor man, or others. I am satisfied that people can live better here than they can in Old England and eat more good Meat.
>
> My love salutes thee. Farewell. Richard Hartshorne, New Jersie, Middleton, September 12, 1675.

Richard Hartshorne's lands extended over the entire Highlands peninsula, or neck as it was termed in contemporary speech, from river to river and as far as Clay Pit Creek in today's Navesink / Locust area about 2,800 acres, including all of Sandy Hook. Hartshorne first encountered land title trouble after Nichol's Monmouth Patent was voided, having in good faith purchased William Goulding's grant as this man never left Long Island and never settled in the Highlands. Having resolved this difficulty, Hartshorne found

In this historical sketch, Lenape Vowavapon and Tocus agree on August 8, 1678, to sell to Richard Hartshorne the hunting, fishing, lumbering, and gathering rights on Sandy Hook for 13 shillings. (This sketch by William Canfield first appeared in Monmouth, Our Indian Heritage *by George H. Moss Jr.)*

himself embroiled in an equally problematic, if not downright dangerous, situation with the local Indians.

A few Lenape natives showed up at Hartshorne's residence after he had built his house, cleared land for farm or pasture, and stocked cattle on Sandy Hook. "The Indians came to my house," he said, "and laid their hands on the post and frame and said that the house was theirs, they never had anything for it and told me if I would not buy the land, I must be gone. . . . They at last told me they would kill my cattle and burn my hay, if I would not buy the land or be gone." After consulting with the local patentees, he found the Indians were correct and that the land would have to be bought from the Indians. The lands were purchased later but that did not end the conflict with the Lenape. Sometime later, after Hartshorne and his men attempted to prevent the Indians from coming onto Sandy Hook to harvest beach plums in late August and September, to fish, and to take cedar lumber for building canoes, the tribesmen threatened Hartshorne's cattle and horses on the Hook, so that he would buy the rights to its resources or simply leave the Hook. Hartshorne then executed a deed whereby the Lenape relinquished their Sandy Hook rights forever in return for 13 shillings. The Lenape tribesmen Vowavapon and Tocus made their marks in the presence of John Stout.

Two conclusions can be drawn from the Hartshorne affairs with the Indians: one, that the Lenape had grown sophisticated in the ways of the Europeans and that they had become quite proficient in expressing themselves in English; and two, that certainly by 1690, some 80 years after meeting Hudson's men in 1609, when Juet noted the presence of an Indian village here, the Lenape had left the waters, beaches, and hills in the Highlands. Now, the Lenape knew what the white man's arrival meant to them.

In 1678, when Richard Hartshorne came and built "Portland" on the other side of the Highlands peninsula or neck, he eventually cleared the Lenape out and cleared the land for fruit, vegetable, and animal raising. Woods of various hardwood and softwood trees, thick and dark, covered all the hills, the home of vast herds of deer. Hartshorne cut a new road through the hills to connect the Highlands beach and Sandy Hook to his home "Portland," on the North Shrewsbury River on the other side. This was "the Portland Road," or just Portland Road of today. One can follow Portland Road in a car from Route 36 / Navesink Avenue up into Hartshorne Woods Park and then, by foot only, down the hill on the other side, following the original road, now a trail, to exit the woods quite near the location of the Hartshorne house. Navesink Avenue, back then, was little more than a Lenape Indian trail, somewhat improved for horses and vehicles, which ran down through Butter Milk Valley through Navesink village and up into and through Chapel Hill to today's Route 35 in Middletown.

3. The Colonial and Revolutionary War Era

Throughout the eighteenth century, the life of a person living in the Highlands was, generally speaking, rather low key. It was a life of farming and fishing, especially for the much-desired oysters and clams so abundant in the bay and rivers. Except for the Hartshornes, probably most residents never ventured beyond the very local area.

The quiet life, however, was interrupted and punctuated by disturbance and violence coming from outside the Highlands: privateers swooping upon the few unsuspecting residents; militia guards manning beacons in the hills; lots of summer fishermen from across the Raritan; countless outbound ships in the Horse Shoe taking on water from the Spout; fear and worry, divided loyalties, Patriot, Loyalist, or neutral in the coming Revolution; shots of battle from the bluff at Esek Hartshorne's place; and the assortment of violence and discontent warfare brings to civilian life.

During the entire eighteenth century, it is impossible to do more than make an educated guess at the number of residents in the Highlands of Navesink. Census reports simply do not exist until 1850, and that year's report is for the entire population of the Township of Middletown. However, it does provide reliable information to estimate the population of Highlands, nonetheless. Prior to this, only population counts of all of Monmouth County or all of the Township of Middletown are available and provide no practical information for Highlands itself.

Contemporary historians do know that Richard Hartshorne settled in Highlands in 1678 on lands which totaled approximately 2,800 acres. The basis of his wealth was in the land, which he held tightly within the family; no outsider purchased Hartshorne lands until 1795. This land produced much, deriving income for the family from farming; from the raising of cattle for milk and meat, of horses, pigs, and sheep; from timber cut from the hills (pine, hickory, and oak) and Sandy Hook (cedar for boat and shipbuilding, worth 200 New York Pounds per year in 1748); and, of course, from hunting and fishing. Assuming a staff of 10 men and 5 women, not all of whom were married, and approximately 10 family members (including Richard, his wife, Margaret, and 12 children, of whom 5 died very young), one may estimate a Highlands population total of 25, living in several houses throughout the hills, at the outset of the century. This number appears correct when compared to the numbers listed in 1870 and 1880 census reports for the Hartshorne estate, when its size was less than half of the original. The population of the entire township of Middletown cited earlier in Richard Hartshorne's promotional

Although this scene depicts Highlands in the nineteenth century, it does capture the rugged and romantic character of the Highlands' geography, one that would be tamed by early settlers like Richard Hartshorne.

letter of September 1675 was 25 families with 95 "lusty" children, totaling approximately 150 people. By 1682, there may have been as many as 100 families and perhaps 500 people.

Occasionally, one encounters reports mentioning houses in Highlands, suggesting a small settlement was in place. For example, from the *Boston News-Letter*, June 28, 1704, a French privateer terrorized the coast and even landed 24 men at the Highlands, where they plundered two houses. Hearing that news, Captain Hamilton ordered a strict guard be kept there as protection from another surprise raid. However, nothing conclusive can be drawn except that the Highlands no doubt had several houses and that the population was large enough to warrant the posting of a citizen militia guard.

It was during Queen Ann's War (1702 to 1713) that the French privateers plagued the New York and Sandy Hook area and the New York General Assembly proposed the erection of a beacon in the Highlands, Sandy Hook, and other places to warn the city of privateers. The assembly suggested three men posted at the Highlands beacon with a powerful and loud, attention-getting cannon always loaded to be fired when the beacon was lighted. Apparently, the beacon warning was ineffective, for during King George's War of 1741 to 1748, the Highlands beacon was accidentally burned down and the flames went unnoticed in New York. The important point to be drawn here is that Highlands was growing in importance in itself and in its relationship to and protection of the city across the bay.

While there is ample evidence pertaining to the agricultural life of the Highlands population, few references to a fishing industry exist, although common sense would suggest an active fishing force given the location of the Highlands, a place literally embraced by the sea. From the *New York Journal or General Advertiser* of April 26, 1770, the following is mentioned: "To be Sold. A plantation in the Township of Middletown, whereon is the Noted Watering Place (*i.e.* Hudson's Spring or the Spout), on the Highlands of Navesinks." The paper noted the plantation had 100 acres, mostly woods; a good house with cellar and kitchen and outbuildings; a fruit orchard of peaches, plums, and cherries; fairly good to grow grain and corn; and "Plenty of Fish and Clams within a small distance from the Door." And most importantly, it was "commodiously situated for a Tavern, as a great Number of Watermen resort there in Summer Season."

The tavern suggests a transient population of travelers and fishermen, seeking meals and refreshment, entertainment and lodging, something typical of the tavern of the day and well illustrated by the eighteenth-century Allen House in Shrewsbury when it was a tavern under the "Sign of the Blue Ball."

As the storm clouds of an approaching violent clash with Britain thickened and darkened over Monmouth County after the ominous events in Boston, Lexington, Concord, and Bunker Hill, people of conscience began to take sides. Perhaps one-third of the Monmouth County population remained overtly loyal to the Crown, with many more tacitly loyal and fearing retaliation. These British sympathizers were called Tories by the Patriots, who themselves were rebels to the British. After July 4, 1776, many Tories fled to New York for safety, having abandoned their homes and farms; others stayed on to resist the rule of the Provincial and Continental Congresses throughout the war, allowing their homes to be havens for marauding Refugees, as displaced Tories came to be known, and reporting Patriot militia movements. Shrewsbury was a hotbed of Tory resistance, Sandy Hook was a haven for Refugee marauders and British sympathizers, and Middletown harbored both Tories and Patriots.

The Battle of Neversink was the first major engagement of British and American forces in Monmouth County during the Revolution. The clash took place on February 13, 1777, when a party of some 170 British troops of the 26th Regiment, commanded by Major Andrew Gordon, met at least five companies of the Monmouth Militia in the vicinity of today's Twin Lights in the area then called Neversink or Nevesink in the Highlands of Neversink.

The following account of the engagement appeared in a letter from a British officer, which was published in the *New York Gazette and Weekly Mercury* on February 24, 1777:

> On Monday last, a Detachment of 170 Men from the 26th Regiment, under Major Gordon, marched from Richmond in Staten Island to Colis' Ferry, where they embarked for Sandy Hook, with the intention of cutting off a party of Rebels stationed at the Highlands of Nevesink.
>
> After being detained on board by hard gale winds and bad weather for three days, they landed (wading up to their waists) on the beach at Highlands, about two miles below the rebel posts. A little before day, they marched and surprised the advanced guard without firing a shot.
>
> From thence they proceeded about a mile further to the house of one Hartshorn, to which they were approaching by two different ways (the flanking companies taking to the right).

The Hartshorne house at issue was the Esek Hartshorne house, taken by the Monmouth Militia as a guard station to cover all movements of the British fleet and Refugees on Sandy Hook. The militia built a strong stone outbuilding to serve as a powder magazine. This was the house that later became Highlands' first hotel, associated with the Water Witch House or Hotel. The article continues to detail the events as follows:

> A guard posted at about 200 yards from the house were first alarmed.
>
> There after firing a few shots together with their main body, who at first affected to form and take a stand, being pushed by the Battalion, fled too soon for the Grenadiers and Light Infantry to come up in time enough to cut off their retreat. Between 30 and 40 escaped.
>
> We found several dead bodies in the woods, which were buried by the soldiers. The whole of the prisoners taken amounting to 72 (amongst which are 2 Captains and 4 Lieutenants) were carried on board the *Syren*.
>
> Many had certificates about them of their having taken the Oaths of Allegiance. Their stores consisted of 2 or 3 barrels of powder, 770 ball cartridges, some salt provision and 9 or 10 quarters of fresh beef, with a light cart and team. The next day, the local people who had met the Fugitives [the Monmouth militia men who escaped] reported that many of them were wounded.

Some indication of the extent of the disaster for Colonel Nathaniel Scudder's First Regiment of Monmouth Militia is to be found in a series of pension applications recorded

The Water Witch Hotel was destroyed by fire in 1875. The fireplace and chimney marked the historic site, which was frequented by tourists until 1918, when Dr. Everett Fields removed the bricks and rebuilt the fireplace in his new home at Marine Place and Water Witch Avenue.

at the Monmouth County Clerk's Office in Freehold between 1779 and 1782. There were applications from widows of three men killed in the fighting and for seven others who died in New York while being held prisoner by the British. They do not indicate where they were being held, but in all probability, the Americans were kept in the infamous Liberty Street Sugar House, where during hot summer weather, as many as a dozen men died each day from disease or poor medical treatment of wounds. Killed in action were Second Lieutenants John Witlock (or Whitlock or Whitelock) and Alexander Clark of Captain Thomas Hunn's company and James Crawford of Captain Samuel Carhart's company. The militiamen who died in prison were as follows: Mathias Rue (on February 28, 1777) and James Hibbits of Captain Kenneth Hankinson's Company; James Winter (on March 11, 1777), Obadiah Stillwell (on April 13, 1777), and William Cole (on March 15, 1778) from Captain Joseph Stillwell's Company; and Lambert Johnson (on April 15, 1777, from smallpox) from Captain Barns Smock's Company.

The county justices who reviewed the pension claims usually approved "half pay due to her husband as the law directs." In the case of militiaman Lambert Johnson's widow, Charity, the half pay was specified as 25 shillings a month.

More than 200 years later, Hamilton Fish, descendant of one of the men involved in the battle, set up on December 6, 1990, a monument in Bayview Cemetery in Leonardo, memorializing James Morris as follows: "James Morris, born January 9, 1754, died October 20, 1820, Patriot, captured by the British February 13, 1777 at Highlands of Navesink, transferred to a ship and then to the Sugar House prison in New York, where he stayed 1777–1778. After release he served until May 20, 1783 in the N.J. Continental line."

Refugee bands who holed up and avoided retaliation in the safety of Sandy Hook would sortie from their haven in raids of plunder, death, and destruction inflicted primarily upon the Patriot homes, farms, and businesses, but at times even upon the pacifist Quakers and Tories and Royalists in places as far away as Shrewsbury, Middletown, and Tinton Falls. Sometimes, the Monmouth County Militia companies would lay in wait in Highlands watching for some Refugee band to leave for or return from one of their infamous raids into the country. This was a very dangerous operation, for at times the Refugees exceeded 200 in number and were as ruthless in defending themselves and their booty as they had been in taking it. By way of retaliation, a band of Refugees lay in wait for the return of Joseph Murray, of the First Battalion Monmouth Militia under Colonel Asher Holmes, to his farm in Middletown, and coming out of the high grass, they murdered him with musket shots and bayonet. He was on leave to plough his fields from his company in Highlands, who were guarding against Refugee movements.

Captain John Schenck of Pleasant Valley (not the man who attacked the Sandy Hook Light) was a staunch supporter of liberty and a promoter and enforcer of the Resolutions for Mutual Protection and Retaliation of Enemies, whereby Tory sympathizers would have their personal and real property seized by Patriots as punishment for their actions. The British put a price on his head: 50 Guineas dead or alive. At one point, the British even tried to bribe him with a large sum of money into relaxing his opposition against the Tories, but this only caused Schenck to exclaim all the louder, "The whole of Europe cannot buy me! Give me liberty!"

On one occasion, Schenck and his company of militia men were down at the Highlands where they fell in with a band of Refugees who had just come over from the Hook to plunder. He informed his superior officer of the raid, but when the officer refused to give the order to attack, Schenck took the responsibility upon himself to order and command a charge. The skirmish resulted in the capture of several horses and 28 Refugees, of whom some dozen were taken away as prisoners. The people of Shrewsbury no doubt slept secure from the worry of attack that night, and the price on brave John Schenck's head went up as well.

Probably the best known, but least accurately reported, historical event to happen in Highlands during the Revolutionary War took place in the summer of 1778. Fearing that France might enter the war on behalf of the Americans (France had on February 6, 1778, officially recognized the independence of the new United States of America), the British decided in early March to unite their two armies, the one occupying Philadelphia, the other holding New York. To ensure their control of New York, especially if confronted with the blockade of the city by a French fleet, the British needed to evacuate Philadelphia and to move their 12,000 troops to New York. Due to a shortage of transport and war ships and the fear of the sudden arrival of hostile French forces from the sea, Sir Henry Clinton, now commanding general of all the military forces, came to Philadelphia from New York on May 8 and departed with his troops on June 18, 1878, on a march across the Jerseys to Sandy Hook. The normal and preferred method of movement of large numbers of troops and their equipment was by ship down the Delaware River around Cape May and up along the Jersey coast and then around Sandy Hook into the harbor at New York. Actually, some of the huge baggage supply, a small number of troops, and incidental non-military

General Sir Henry Clinton (1738–1795) began military service in the New York Militia, served in Germany in the Seven Years' War, and distinguished himself at the Battle of Bunker Hill in 1775. For his service in the Battle of Long Island in 1776, he was knighted and made lieutenant general. When Howe resigned his command, Clinton advanced to chief of all British forces in 1778 and decided to move his troops from Philadelphia to New York, setting the stage for the Battle of Monmouth.

personnel had been dispatched to New York by the sea route before the rest of the army set out across the Jerseys.

It was on June 28, 1778, which happened to be the most unbearably hot and humid day imaginable, that the two opposing generals finally came head on against one another with all their might in the Battle of Monmouth. While the two sides essentially fought to a draw, fighting from dawn until just as the sun went down, the loss of men on both sides amounted to some 500 soldiers, probably 200 under Washington and 300 under Clinton.

The reason Clinton made for New York via Sandy Hook was twofold. First, a direct march north for the city would have taken his army through territory more hostile than that of Burlington and Monmouth Counties in New Jersey, and it would ultimately require ship passage across the Hudson River. Second, Sandy Hook had been, since the start of the war, a safe haven, easily defended, for British forces. In fact, since the British military fleet arrived off Sandy Hook on June 29, 1776, large numbers of Monmouth County British sympathizers, called "Loyalists" by themselves and the British, called "traitorous scum" by the Monmouth County Patriots, fled to Sandy Hook and fortified it with British military and financial assistance.

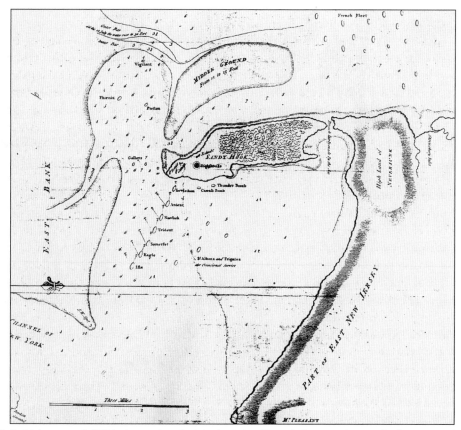

A British map of 1778 shows Sandy Hook "island" and the "High Land of Neversunk," where British General Henry Clinton's troops embarked for passage to New York after the Battle of Monmouth, June 28, 1778.

The two armies met in the fields of Manalapan near Freehold, county seat of Monmouth County. It was Sunday, June 28, 1778, when they fought to a virtual draw in the Battle of Monmouth. It was more of a psychological victory and boost to the American soldiers and to the Continental Congress, which was at times dilatory in financing Washington's requests. This military draw also proved that the supposed rag-tag American colonial army had become a formidable weapon under General Washington's command against the highly professional military forces of Great Britain. News of the success at Monmouth was expected to encourage greater and continued support from the European powers.

To call the excursion of Clinton's army from Freehold to Sandy Hook a British "retreat," implying that he was running away from the American army after having suffered a defeat or serious blow, is simply wrong and clearly the result of anti-British propaganda distorting the historical record. Clinton did not alter his course toward Sandy Hook in any way—except to divide his troops into two units, the one under General Wilhelm von Knyphausen, which set out immediately, and the other under his own command, which set out three hours later on the route north. Whether there had been a battle with Washington or not in Freehold or any other place, he had long before carefully planned his route from Philadelphia to Highlands and the Hook.

Fortunately, the "Road the Army Marched" survives on a map bearing this caption probably created at the time by John Hills, who was with Clinton's army. On modern Route 36 (still called Navesink Avenue in Highlands) at the ocean, some of the British troops went down today's Linden Avenue and Water Witch Avenue to Gravelly Point, where the deepwater near shore allowed large transports to ferry troops and equipment over to Sandy Hook. Others went on along Route 36 / Navesink Avenue to the area north of the present Highlands–Sea Bright bridge, where the British Navy had hastily constructed a pontoon bridge across the inlet recently opened by the forces of a severe storm, effectively making Sandy Hook an island cut off from the Highlands mainland.

Although Clinton's forces reached the Highlands the day after the battle, they waited a few days before crossing from Highlands to Sandy Hook and then to New York. This was necessitated by the need to gather boats and materials for the Navy's construction of the bridge across the inlet at the base of the Hook, which allowed ocean water to rush into the bay. During these five days, the troops were encamped in the hills running from Garrett and Chapel Hills to Navesink and the Highlands proper. Lord Cornwallis was quartered in the large Garrett Hill house.

This location vanished from the map once the Earle Naval Depot took over the area in WW II. Today, its only relic is the modern street called Garrett Hill Road, which runs south from Leonardville Road just two streets west of the Earle Naval Pier bridge crossing in Belford. The Garrett Hill house belonged to John Taylor, whose wife and family were still in residence; Taylor was absent on militia duty. Cornwallis's officers were situated in other houses such as the Stillwell house on Chapel Hill (off today's Stillwell Road), with the troops and camp followers encamped in the woods on the nearby slopes. Both these houses gave a clear and unobstructed view of the bay and Hook, thus providing the military commanders information of the progress of work for crossing to the Hook. Both

The Captain Joshua Huddy monument is now located in Highlands' Huddy Park just 100 yards from where Huddy had been hanged on April 12, 1782.

the American and British generals knew the British were secure from enemy attack in these totally unassailable hills.

The following bronze inscription is set in a rough granite stone placed on the edge of Huddy Park in Highlands to honor Joshua Huddy, called the hero martyr of Monmouth: "Here / Captain Joshua Huddy / of the Monmouth County Artillery / a Prisoner of War / Captured March 24 1782 while defending / the Blockhouse at Toms River / was hung by Tories without Warrant / April 12, 1782. / The British authorities repudiated / but did not atone for that Crime. / The Sons of the Revolution in New Jersey / have set up this stone to the / Memory of the Patriotic Victim."

Joshua Huddy was a staunch partisan in the Revolutionary cause. He became a popular hero in his time for his conspicuous bravery and his dashing exploits. Huddy served as a captain in the militia and was authorized to raise and command an artillery company in the Monmouth County Militia. His unit served at the Battle of Monmouth under General David Forman.

The Refugees wreaked havoc on the homes, farms, and businesses of Patriots, plundering, burning, and looting, only to disappear into the protection of thick woods, swamps, river, and coastal islands. They were vigilantly observed, ruthlessly harassed, and continually pursued by Huddy and his company. Thus, Huddy became a revered, almost legendary protector and figure of romance to the Patriots and an infamous object of scorn and hatred to the Loyalists and Tory Refugees. Huddy was a wanted man, wanted dead but preferably alive to be made an example. Of the several attempts to get Huddy, one was made on September 1, 1780, when a gang of Refugees and renegades headed by "Colonel Tye" (actually a black runaway slave named Titus) swept down to Colts Neck and surrounded his house near today's Colts Neck Inn.

That night, the house, usually a station of Huddy's militia company, was unprotected and at the mercy of the besieging Refugees. His wife, Catherine, begged Huddy to surrender but he, the fox, leaped to action, firing the many muskets kept in the house from different windows as Catherine and a slave girl named Lucretia Emmons reloaded the weapons, giving the impression that several men defended the house and even wounding a few including Colonel Tye, who later died of his wound.

The Refugees decided to torch the house and burn Huddy out, shooting all the occupants as they fled. Huddy surrendered on the condition they not burn the house. Having taken Huddy captive, the Refugees began to plunder the house but were interrupted and prevented by the arrival of half a dozen militia men summoned by neighbors who heard the shooting.

Quickly the Refugees fled with Huddy, running overland until coming to their boats left concealed at Black Point at the end of the Rumson peninsula. They were exhilarated with their capture of the fox Huddy; their mood changed, however, once they realized that they were being pursued by a pack of militiamen who fired from the beach, killing five of them and accidentally wounding Huddy in the thigh. Huddy slipped overboard into the water, swimming and yelling to them, "I am Huddy! I am Huddy!" Huddy recovered from his wound. The Refugees did not; it festered in them as they plotted and sought another opportunity to get Huddy. Two years later their chance came at last.

That chance, however, came some six months after the surrender of Cornwallis at Yorktown, Virginia, on October 17, 1781. During this interval, hostilities still continued, for there was not yet an armistice or treaty of surrender agreed upon. The situation of the Tories and Refugees in Monmouth County was critical; they were in deep despair and plagued with uncertainty about their future and with bitterness toward the British, having been virtually abandoned without resources despite their loyalty to the Crown. They were

The Colts Neck home of Captain Joshua Huddy appears here in an 1840 sketch. This residence is where Huddy had been attacked and captured by Refugees, soon embittered by his daring escape at Black Point, Rumson. A monument in the park near the Rumson–Sea Bright bridge marks this action.

a nationless lot surrounded by an enemy majority whom they had betrayed and by whom they were now despised. This hopelessness and rage led the Refugees and surviving Tories to acts of vengeance.

Early in 1782, Huddy was stationed in command of some 25 men at the blockhouse and stockade located at Toms River in lower Monmouth County. Monmouth extended all along the bayshore and down just north of Tuckerton. In 1850, Ocean County was created from lower Monmouth. This post was an important one in order to protect the salt flats and works that produced the salt vital for the preservation of fish and meat in the days before refrigeration.

At daybreak on Sunday, March 24, 1782, a force of some 120 Loyalists from a group in Pennsylvania, Refugees, and some of the infamous Pine Robbers from the nearby wilderness arrived in boats and surrounded the blockhouse. Huddy's men were badly outnumbered and the attackers demanded their surrender. Huddy refused, calling out a defiant, "Come and take us!" The enemy did just that, but only after Huddy's men put up a gallant defense. With their shot and powder exhausted, Huddy's men fought on with pikes against the enemy as they climbed the walls. Finally, they Refugees took the blockhouse, finding nine Monmouth men dead. In their cruel frenzy, the Refugees shot or bayoneted some of Huddy's men after they surrendered. Next, the enemy burned the stockade, the houses in the town, and all the mills and saltworks. They dragged off 11 Patriot defenders as prisoners, with Captain Joshua Huddy as their prize, taking them to New York City's infamous Sugar House prison.

On Monday, April 8, 1782, Huddy and two of the men captured with him were transferred by sloop to the British man-o-war *Britannia*, anchored within the Horse Shoe of Sandy Hook. It was Tory militia Captain Richard Lippincott originally of Shrewsbury who had Huddy brought out of New York to the ship within sight of the Highlands. Perhaps with a sarcastic smile, one of the Refugees informed Huddy, who was in chains in the hold of the ship, that he was to be hanged for the torture, mutilation, and murder of Philip White. At this, Huddy protested that the charge was false to the members of the Board of Associated Loyalists, asserting correctly that White had been killed after Huddy had been taken prisoner. "Prepare to be hanged immediately!" was their only response.

Huddy was fast delivered up to Richard Lippincott and rowed by Loyalists and British sailors to Gravelly Point in Highlands to be hanged on Monmouth County soil as a warning and deliberate act of vengeance to his Monmouth County men. While they prepared the gallows, Huddy was allowed time to prepare himself and compose his last will. They stood Huddy on a barrel under the branch of a tree near the same roadway Clinton's soldiers had marched on some four years before as they sought New York via Sandy Hook after the Battle of Monmouth. At Lippincott's command, the barrel was kicked away and Captain Joshua Huddy passed into eternity and liberty.

Huddy's body was left suspended from the rope attached to the tree. They knew the local patriots would find it along this commonly traveled road. In a pocket was Huddy's will and across his chest was a placard: "Up Goes Huddy for Philip White." They knew their message would be relayed loud and its meaning understood very clearly to their enemies throughout Monmouth County.

Sandy Hook Lighthouse, the nation's oldest lighthouse continually in use, dates to June 11, 1764. During the Revolutionary War, it was the center of British Refugee Town and the object of American militia attacks. (Courtesy Lola Adolf.)

The tree was not located in today's Huddy Park, a public area dedicated to his memory at a ceremony during the nation's bicentennial in 1976, at which time the bronze-granite monument was moved from the site of his death to the park. The tree, reputed to have been a very large basswood tree, stood as late as 1895 and is very prominently marked on a map of Water Witch Park as the "Joshua Huddy Tree." At that time, the continuation of Linden Avenue across Water Witch Avenue (today sometimes called South Linden Avenue) was named "Huddy Lane" on the same map. The Sons of the Revolution in New Jersey set their monument on the site of the tree. Several archival photographs show the monument set off and surrounded by a low iron piping fence and situated on the side of Water Witch Avenue opposite the park, approximately 100 feet uphill from the old Central Railroad of New Jersey tracks (today's Shore Drive).

Patriot William Schenck of the Highlands of Navesink section of Middletown served the Revolutionary cause bravely when he led a band of Monmouth men in an attempt to darken the beacon light on Sandy Hook. The Sandy Hook Lighthouse, the oldest lighthouse in continuous use in North America, was erected in 1762 and first lighted on June 11, 1764. It is on record that the New York Congress on March 4, 1776, resolved to have the tower, and thus the beacon, destroyed as a protection against a successful arrival of the British fleet, a happening feared and expected each day by New York and New Jersey Patriots. Of course, the Sandy Hook Light was the critical element in the fleet's safe nighttime approach to the city. A Major Malcolm was charged with dismantling the lens, taking care to preserve the glass, and with taking the lamps and oil supply for the light. He did manage to remove the lamps and oil, taking them to the Highlands mainland and

31

Philip Freneau was a sailor, soldier, scholar, editor, and "Poet of the Revolution." He lived at Middletown Point (today's Matawan). While serving with the First Regiment of the Monmouth Militia on guard at the Highlands during the war, he was attacked by Refugees leaving Sandy Hook.

turning them over to Patriot officer Colonel George Taylor, whose house stood atop Garrett Hill in Middletown. This house became the headquarters of Lord Cornwallis on June 29 through July 4 or 5, 1778, after the Battle of Monmouth. Taylor, later in the war, was terribly mistrusted by the American Patriots and was considered a Tory in disguise due to his "too equal" treatment of men of both sides in the dispute.

Apparently, the British forces were able to maintain the beacon throughout the years of the Revolutionary War, perhaps only briefly extinguishing it at a time in 1778, when they had fears of a French fleet's arrival off New York. The peninsula, which occasionally became an island, was quite heavily fortified by regular British troops, and a large band of rugged "Refugees" maintained a Sandy Hook stronghold centered around the cannon-proof lighthouse tower from the first shot fired in the Revolution well past the surrender of Cornwallis and the later evacuation of the British and their Loyalist supporters from New York.

Yet this did not discourage Lieutenant William (or John, as the sources vary) Schenck, the father of Peter W. Schenck and his son Peter F. Schenck of Highlands (both important and influential men who played significant roles in farming and land development and Shrewsbury River crossings either by ferry or bridge). Lieutenant Schenck took his band of local Patriot warriors in boats across from Gravelly Point, under the cover of darkness, and landed on the bay beach. There, they knocked the lantern of the light to pieces, leaving a dent in the iron of the lens—the mark of their 6-pound cannonball so accurately aimed at the beacon light.

After the war, perhaps as a reward for his leadership in the brave and daring action, Schenck became the first keeper of the light, serving from 1809 until his death in 1817.

This was at a time when lighthouse keeper positions were typically political appointments coming out of the county government in Freehold.

Philip Morin Freneau has often been termed the Poet Patriot of the American Revolution. In the years prior to the outbreak of war, he ceaselessly turned out articles and poems from his home near Middletown Point (now Matawan) promoting the cause of independence. Early on, he served on privateer vessels preying on British shipping, during which time he received a bullet wound in the knee. After the Battle of Monmouth, Freneau enlisted as a private in the First Regiment of the Monmouth Militia, which performed scout and guard duty along the shore, especially near Highlands. It was here that Freneau was involved in a tangle with Refugees in which he personally was assaulted and his dog, Sancho, took a saber wound to the head and died.

Leaving the militia as a sergeant, he again went to sea aboard a privateer vessel, was captured by the British, and sentenced to prison aboard the prison ship *Scorpion* and the hospital ship *Hunter*. Suffering unimaginable hardship, disease, and privation, he was released in a prisoner exchange in July 1780. His experiences he memorialized in his long poem "The British Prison Ship."

Freneau immortalized the Highlands with the following poem entitled "Neversink," which he composed on the hills of Neversink near Sandy Hook in 1790.

These hills the pride of all the coast
To mighty distance seen,
With aspect bold and rugged brow,
That shade the neighboring main;
These heights for solitude designed,
This rude, resounding shore,
These vales impervious to the wind,
Tall oaks, that to the tempest bend,
Half Druid, I adore.

From distant lands a thousand sails,
Your hazy summits greet,
You saw the angry Briton come,
You saw him, last, retreat!
With towering crest you first appear
The news of land to tell;
To him that comes, fresh joys impart,
To him that goes, a heavy heart,
The lover's long farewell.

'Tis yours to see the sailor bold,
Of persevering mind,
To see him rove in search of care,
And leave true bliss behind:

To see him spread his flowing sails
To trace a tiresome road;
By wintry seas and tempests chased,
To see him o'er the ocean haste,
A comfortable abode!

Your thousand springs of water blue
What luxury to sip,
As from the mountain's breast they flow
To moisten Flora's lip!
In vast retirements herd the deer,
Where forests round them rise,
Dark groves their tops in ether lost,
That, haunted still by Huddy's ghost,
The trembling rustic flies.

Proud heights! with pains so often seen
(With joy beheld once more),
On your firm base I take my stand,
Tenacious of the shore;
Soft sleep and ease, blest days and nights,
And health, attend these favorite heights,
Retirement's blest abode!

During most of the years of the Revolutionary War, the house of the Quaker Esek Hartshorne, built in 1762, was occupied by Patriot troops. The Hartshornes, being Quakers, took no part in the dispute with the British and because their neutrality was based on religious principles, the Hartshornes suffered no physical, economic, or social retaliation from either side. The residence was built in an ideal location on a slight slope along the bluff that affords today a magnificent vista and back then a commanding view of New York, all Raritan Bay and Sandy Hook, and Long Island beyond. From here, all British Navy and Refugee movements could be observed. A small stone house, with thick walls, was built adjacent to the house to serve as a powder and shot magazine to supply the surrounding militia men. The house stood on the north part of the block formed by Navesink Avenue, Rogers Street, South Linden Avenue, and Waddell Street.

After Esek died in 1795, his executors sold his 800-acre estate in 1797 to Tylee (or Tyler) Williams, who in 1798 sold an undivided half interest in the tract to Nimrod Woodward. He took over the house and operated it as a hotel for many years, well into the next century. Woodward was not taking a risk and leaping into uncharted business territory by starting up a Highlands hotel. As early 1722, an inn or tavern was located at Black Point on Rumson Neck. In 1752, John Hartshorne and his wife, Lucy, operated the inn, which later appeared on the 1851 Lightfoot map of Monmouth County. It was well known enough to make the *Philadelphia Gazette* in 1767, "the noted Tavern at Black Point, Shrewsbury, Monmouth County." In 1814, the inn was up for sale and advertised in the *New York Post* of October 14 as "the Inn is so well known to Philadelphia and New York

Highlands' first hotel, originally the Esek Hartshorne house, was built in 1762 and was the site of the Battle of Neversink in 1777.

that it is not necessary to enter into a particular description." A modern Black Point Inn exists in Rumson, but not on the same site.

Another inn is thought to have existed by 1812, when Thomas Martin built and ran a tavern or inn on Spermaceti Cove on Sandy Hook, which came to be known as the Cove House, said to have been frequented by Sandy Hook pilots. It supposedly burned in the winter of 1854 or 1855. Interpretive officials at Gateway National Recreation Area's Sandy Hook Unit claim to have found physical evidence pertaining to the inn's structure, size, and location on the edge of the cove not far from the present-day visitors center.

While the establishment and operation of inns or hotels in the Highlands and nearby areas are reliable evidence of a traveling public in need of accommodations, one must be careful not to exaggerate the extent of the demand at a time when it would of necessity be limited by the availability of transportation to the area. Before the advent of reliable steamboat transportation from New York City to the Highlands and other stops along the rivers, visitors had to make use of the slow-moving and unpredictable sailing sloops or packet boats, which existed primarily for the purpose of moving to the large city markets fresh produce from the farms in the interior of the county and seafood, especially clams and oysters, from the rivers and bay. Typically, passengers aboard these boats meant extra income to the boat captains and owners (and sometimes a nuisance, as well).

There were, however, passenger sloops exclusively for the traveling public, but these, according to the recollections of Tabor Chadwick, keeper of the Twin Lights, were unreliable. "In 1812 one might get to New York by taking either of two lines or river packets which left the wharves [probably at today's Red Bank] on Tuesday, returning on the following Friday, provided that wind and tide and Providence proved auspicious."

War and its subsequent dangers also adversely affected the size of the traveling public. Thus, during the entire time of the Revolutionary War, from 1776 through 1783, it must have been safer to stay in New York than to suffer the risks of travel to Highlands and the rest of Monmouth County, even given the tight British fleet's control of the waters crossed. Likewise, during the second war with Britain, from 1812 through 1814, water travel in both directions must have been restricted out of fear, despite the protection afforded by the American warships blockading the entrance to the lower harbor.

Nonetheless, the establishment and successful operation of the Woodward Hotel is a certain indication of a nascent interest in the Highlands by travelers, if not tourists, from the city. Thus, the year 1798 marks the beginning of tourism in Highlands, and this industry grew steadily throughout the nineteenth and twentieth centuries and continues still today at the dawn of the twenty-first.

4. The Nineteenth Century through the Civil War

For the people of Highlands, the period of the nineteenth century was one of almost constant, fast-paced change brought about by economic and social forces beyond their ability to resist or control and coming into their lives from well outside the narrow limits of their little community.

Wars unsettled their lives. In 1812, all the Highlands was an armed camp of militia soldiers and cannons, with British prowling the waters. Twenty Highlands men and boys went off to Union regiments in the Civil War, some more than once, leaving worried wives and mothers. Cannons roared over on Sandy Hook as guns were tested. One fort in the Civil War was never completed; then, another burst into existence at the end of the century, due to the war with Spain, and it was the size of the town of Red Bank, and located at the end of the Hook.

The war between the United States and Great Britain, caused by the British outrages upon American shipping and sailors and being primarily a maritime war, quite naturally involved the Highlands due to its strategic location overlooking Sandy Hook, the lower harbor, and the approaches to New York City from the open sea. Even before the formal declaration of war on June 19, 1812, a large number of troops, several rifle companies and an artillery company, was stationed in the Highlands. John Thompson and Samuel Van Schanck were two local men in service during the war. A report dated March 31, 1813, speaks of the Highlands post as having been strengthened with five full companies of artillery and three of riflemen. The fort there was equipped with several 32-pound cannons and some 800 troops of the Jersey Blues encamped on the Highlands. Barracks and blockhouses were constructed by a special force of 280 workmen (Highlands men included) brought in especially for this task. To bolster the Highlands fort, 200 troops of the New Jersey Militia were dispatched there on May 11, 1813.

After the Highlands work was completed, the same 280-man workforce started fortifications on Sandy Hook in March 1813. The fort was located about half a mile north of the lighthouse and just south of the granite Civil War fort, a portion of which still survives today in the Coast Guard area. It was more of a stockade than a real fortress, having been constructed hastily out of wood.

Fortunately, there was only a single hostile action that took place in Sandy Hook Bay: the successful capture of the small British sloop *Eagle* by Americans disguised as fishermen on July 4, 1813. On the mainland around Highlands, not a musket or cannon was fired

This 1979 oil painting by Marge Ehringer illustrates the original 1828 Twin Lights and keeper's quarters.

against an enemy except perhaps as a signal to alert the guard. Nonetheless, there was a real threat and a great worry of an invasion of coastal locations from ships, as happened on the Potomac with the invasion of Washington and the burning of the President's mansion on August 24, 1814. Closer to home, there is a report that somehow a British cruiser fired its cannons and two of the shells wound up in the grounds around the Hartshorne property on the Navesink River, the other side of the peninsula from the Highlands. The British maintained a rather tight blockade of New York Harbor and even made an occasional show of force in approaching the channel to the city. Apparently, the fortifications on the Hook and in the Highlands, along with gunboats in the bay and lower harbor, sufficed to deter the British. Nonetheless, worried minds were kept on edge with the memory of the full British occupation of New York, Sandy Hook, and Sandy Hook Bay during six long years in the last war.

Since 1524, when Verrazzano first saw the hills later to support the Twin Lights, this landscape stood as a bold landmark for navigation and the logical site to build a powerful nighttime beacon for ships approaching the treacherous entrance into New York Harbor.

The first Twin Lights were erected in 1827–1828 and fired under the first keeper, named Joshua or Joseph Doty, appointed on April 28, 1828. The lighthouse property of approximately 3 acres had been purchased by the United States government for $600 from Nimrod Woodward. The identical octagonal towers of blue split stone rose 240 and 246 feet above sea level with the south tower being erected on higher ground. In the 320-foot space between the towers was a small wooden keeper's house. The beacon light in each tower was fed by several lard oil flames. However, the lights were not of equal brilliance (*i.e.* not quite twin lights); the north light was stationary of first-order brightness, while the south tower had a revolving light of second-order brightness. The total cost was $10,290.

An improvement of major proportions came in 1841, when the south tower beacon received a French-made Fresnel lens, giving a dramatic extension to the reach of the light across the sea and making it more powerful than its first-order sister in the north tower. While the lights were superior, as early as 1857, inspectors found the supporting stone towers were quickly deteriorating due to inferior construction materials and workmanship and ordered their replacement. Highlands men, doubtless, found employment in the site preparation and construction of the 1827–1828 Twin Lights, assisting the unloading of barges and transport of stones up the original front road to the building site.

As far back as 1746, the hill on which stand today's Twin Lights was the site of the first long-distance communication system in America (long before Paul Revere's "one, if by land and two, if by sea"). Here was placed a beacon, put up at the request and expense of the New York Merchants Association, which was to warn authorities in New York City of the approach of enemy French vessels during the war between France and England.

Because of the elevation of the hill, plus any small tower located on it, being some 240 feet above the level of the sea, a trained observer armed with a powerful telescope could easily discern and identify a ship on the horizon many miles from the tip of Sandy Hook and the entrance into New York, thus affording an ample period of time for the city authorities to prepare a defense.

A signaling system called a telegraph (writing at a distance, according to its Greek etymology, and not to be confused with the electric or magnetic telegraph that Samuel Morse perfected) used large balls hoisted up a 100-foot-high pole during the day and flaming pots of oil during the night. These were used according to a prearranged code system. There were four signal sites: Twin Lights hill in Highlands, the end of Sandy Hook, Staten Island at the Narrows, and the Battery in New York. Reports were read by

This wood engraving from Frank Leslie's Illustrated Newspaper *on September 20, 1856, shows the north tower of the 1828 Twin Lights and the semaphore/telegraph used by marine observer Charles Havens to announce ship arrivals by relay to Manhattan.*

telescope and then relayed along the route. Unfortunately, the system was not perfect, and no doubt at times signals went unnoticed. No matter, for the war with France ended in 1748 and the telegraph was removed.

There is some evidence that a lighthouse may have been built on the same site in 1762, again no doubt paid for by the New York merchants to help guide ships into the channels leading to the city. Such a light would have a greater reach out to sea, due to the elevation of the lens, than the one at Sandy Hook, and between the two lights, an approaching ship, long before taking on a Sandy Hook pilot, would better be able to situate itself in the proper channel.

During the War of 1812, the visual telegraph was reactivated, this time to warn the city authorities and merchants of the approach of British vessels, and proved to be a useful warning device several times—no doubt alleviating some of the anxiety from the population of the city.

In 1829, the Merchants Exchange Company of New York paid to have the old telegraph reactivated and efficiently operated, after having received permission from the Treasury Department to operate the system "on the public ground near the lighthouse at the Highlands of Navesink." Later engravings and an early photograph of the first Twin Lights site show the telegraph operation (a semaphore, at the time) actually on the government grounds located between the two towers. This was quite a concession, for the next time signaling equipment was allowed to be set up on the grounds was 1899, when Marconi erected his gigantic wire antenna there.

In 1834, the Merchants Exchange installed a semaphore telegraph in all the key locations. On a tower about 70 feet high, there was an observation and telegraph room. The agent on duty would scan the horizon watching for an expected ship to break the horizon. He could read its identity from its size, rigging, and from signal flags in the ship's rigging using his powerful telescope. The agent would then move a dial with the numbers 1 to 10 and the words "look out" and "repeat." If he dialed a number from 1 to 6, the upper arm on the semaphore above the shack's roof would move to the corresponding number. If he dialed 7 to 10 or either word, the lower arm would move correspondingly. Each ship of the Merchants Exchange would have its own four-digit code number that was registered in the "Telegrapher's Dictionary." For example, if the ship *Napoleon* were sighted, the operator would dial up 6-3-3-5, which would be relayed to Sandy Hook, to Staten Island at the Narrows, and to the Exchange building's roof in less than 60 seconds!

Today, it might be hard to understand why the system was important back then. In the days of sails, many a ship laden with valuable goods would not make the port of New York, perhaps sunk or damaged and driven off course by storms. It was a great relief for the merchants to know their ships and cargo had arrived safely, and they wanted to know this as soon as possible. The New York newspapers, hotels, and city families wanted to know of the safe arrival of passengers who were guests or family. One forgets today that from the time a sailing ship broke the horizon to the time it finally docked in Manhattan as much as 72 hours could elapse, given the need to wait on the proper disposition of winds and tides.

The first operator of the telegraph was Charles R. Havens, who came to Highlands from Shelter Island at age 21 in 1834. Havens was considered a brilliant and dedicated agent, even if somewhat eccentric, in the opinion of the companies he worked for and of all Highlanders and visitors who knew him. He retired in 1884 from the Western Union Company at full salary in appreciation for his half century of expert service as a marine observer. He died April 8, 1899, but in his last 15 years, he enjoyed still coming to the Twin Lights and telling visitors of the way things were in the old days. His son Vinton was an adept sound telegrapher who took over his father's position for many years. Another son, Arthur, was the first Western Union telegrapher at the Atlantic Highlands train station. The "dits and dahs" and the spark of telegraphy were in their blood.

In 1853, the Morse telegraph first arrived in Highlands at the Twin Lights Marine Observation station, and Charles Havens learned the new apparatus quickly, and the semaphore signaling device (but not the tower structure) was replaced by a paper-recording electric telegraph operated by Havens for the New York and Highlands Telegraph Company. The next year, telegraph wires were stretched across the Shrewsbury River from Twin Lights to Sandy Hook by the New York and Sandy Hook Telegraph Company (later it absorbed the New York and Highlands Telegraph Co.), thus linking the Sandy Hook marine agent to the station at the Twin Lights and then onward to New York City's Merchant Exchange building. Ship arrival news traveled almost at the speed of light along the wires, making Highlands and Sandy Hook well publicized in the day's papers and almost a household word around the metropolitan area.

Today, newspapers like the *Asbury Park Press* are filled with copies of far-away stories supplied by news services such as the Associated Press (AP), Reuters, Gannett News Service, or even the Health and Fitness News Service. Older readers may remember UPI (United Press International) as well. These items used to arrive at the *Press* on noisy paper-printing teletype machines, now relegated to the museum by the miracle of silent operating electronic computers. However, just after the arrival of Samuel Morse's telegraph, the gathering and reporting of news, especially from abroad in Europe, was not such an easy affair.

America was isolated from news from Europe, separated as it was by over 3,000 miles of Atlantic Ocean. A sailing ship leaving Liverpool, England, might take as much as 15 to 20 days to arrive at a dock in the port of New York. World events such as the 1815 defeat of Napoleon's armies by Wellington at Waterloo, vital to American political and financial welfare, failed to reach American government officials, investors, and the common newspaper reader without long delays.

A Highlands man named James Farrell was a key player in a difficult and sometimes dangerous news service operated from Sandy Hook and Highlands Twin Lights hill using the surrounding water and air. Around 1854, shortly after the first telegraph line linked the Highlands with New York City, the wires were extended across the Shrewsbury River from the Twin Lights hill to the end of Sandy Hook. Whenever an inbound vessel was sighted by a powerful telescope and was identified as bearing news reports from Europe, "newsman" James Farrell launched his surf boat and rowed or sailed out to meet the ship, no matter how rough the conditions of the sea or sky above.

News reports had already been prepared in Europe and written in abbreviated form on tissue papers. These were placed in a special water-tight container and thrown over board, marked with a buoy-flag, to await retrieval by Farrell. He attached each news report to the leg of carrier pigeon "Dickie," or one of several birds that he released to fly away rapidly to its coop on Sandy Hook. Here, another agent took the messages and telegraphed them to New York City, where the latest news from Europe was spread across the pages of the *New York Herald*. Its owner and publisher, James Gordon Bennett, initiated this unusual news-gathering service and generally is credited with being the first publisher to make extensive use of the telegraph to gather and report domestic news stories from all parts of America. He personally visited and inspected this news operation when he came to Highlands by steamboat and spent some days of business and pleasure at the old Thompson House Pavilion, situated along the Shrewsbury just below the Twin Lights.

This old news service came to an end after the laying of the first transatlantic telegraph cable in 1858. This rather inefficient cable was replaced with an improved 1866 cable. New York in America and London and other world capitals in Europe became as close as the clicks of a telegrapher's key speeding dots and dashes of news information on the wire cable under the ocean between the two continents.

With these new innovations of communication, Dickie and the other winged messengers went into retirement in Farrell's backyard in lower Highlands. Farrell later went to work as an agent for the Western Union Telegraph Company with sites on Sandy Hook and the Twin Lights, where he spent long, cold days watching the seas for ships.

Farrell never forgot his old co-worker, Dickie, the news pigeon, and often repeated to visitors how little Dickie was often a bit obstinate and filled with his own self importance. He would regularly annoy Farrell's assistant on Sandy Hook by walking around the tower coop keeping just out of reach of his eager hand. "Come on, Dickie, be nice, come here," coaxed the agent. And the bird would coo and coo, as if to answer, "What's the rush, what's the hurry?" Little did Dickie understand that the *Herald* and all America, eager for news from Europe, waited upon the caprices of little Dickie, the news service carrier pigeon.

Pioneer newsman and Highlander James Farrell (c. 1855) kept pigeons and used them in relays of news from ships arriving from Europe to be telegraphed on Sandy Hook to James Gordon Bennett's New York Herald.

The Colonel William Jones Navesink Hotel was originally the Woodward Hotel, which was bought by Jones, a former sheriff of New York. His daughter, Angeline, ran a school for Highlands children in a room in the hotel and later a separate building from 1847 to 1866.

Steamboats and railroads came filled with fancy-dressed visitors, excursionists, tourists—all the same, outsiders!—with money to spend in the big hotels on the river. Then came the theater people from New York, with homes built like castles or palaces in the hills. The new Twin Lights, just grand, and the bridges on the Shrewsbury brought work but more crowds of visitors, too. The resort at Highland Beach spilled over into town and made Highlands its annex. Magazine writers, artists, and photographers advertised the Highlands, with a novel and poetry written about the place, and made things—worse. They wrote about them, there in Parkertown, and made fun of them living, as they did, honest, independent, and hard-working lives on the water as clammers and fishermen, brave men in the Life Saving service, too. And immigrants came too, poor people, rowdy folk, and Catholic Irish.

Sometime just prior to 1812, Nimrod Woodward gained possession of the old Esek Hartshorne property, about 170 acres between the river and Mountain and North Peak Streets. He built the White House, the first hotel along the river in what is today's bridge area, where almost all of the great hotels were located in later years. The exact location was under the concrete abutment of the present 1932 bridge. He and his family ran the hotel until his death in 1829; then in 1830, the hotel and the 170-acre property were sold to Peter W. Schenck, who ran the hotel, enlarging it in 1841, and kept the Schenck Hotel running until 1849, when he leased it to Joseph I. Thompson (keeper of the Twin Lights from 1844 to 1850 and Monmouth County sheriff), who ran the business until 1851.

The Woodward family operated their hotel, the old Esek Hartshorne residence, until about 1840, when it was purchased by a Mrs. Stewart of New York City and run successfully by her managers for about seven years. In 1847, Colonel William Jones, the sheriff of New York, relocated his family to Highlands, where he purchased the hotel from Mrs. Stewart and immediately remodeled and expanded it at a cost of $5,000 to accommodate more than 200 guests. This investment is another indication of the increasing popularity of Highlands as a summer tourist destination.

The Colonel William Jones Navesink Hotel was prominently displayed on the 1851 Lightfoot map of Monmouth County. Jones retired from the hotel business after having entrusted the house, business, and surrounding 100 acres to his son-in-law, Robert N. Waddell, on August 18, 1854. After Jones's death on September 8, 1864, the hotel and all the property were put up for auction on May 22, 1866; Gilbert Giles bought it and about 75% of the property. Giles ran the hotel, actively featuring it as the Water Witch Hotel of James Fenimore Cooper's famous story. On October 9, 1875, the hotel burned to the ground, leaving behind just cinders and the massive fireplace and chimney structure. Afterwards, the ruins themselves were a tourist attraction, being pointed out by local guides who recounted parts of the novel to inquiring tourists. In 1918, while most of the bricks were still safe from souvenir hunters, local summer Highlander Dr. Everett Fields removed the bricks and personally reconstructed the fireplace in his home on the corner of Marine Place and Water Witch Avenue, where they are preserved even today.

A hotelier named Hartman purchased 8 acres of land south of the Schenck hotel in 1851 and constructed the Atlantic Pavilion next to Schenck's Hotel, which he then immediately sold to Joseph I. Thompson, who named it Thompson's Atlantic Pavilion, commonly called the Thompson House, accommodating 300 guests in 1852 and perhaps 200 more in an annex built after the Civil War.

Thompson and his family ran the hotel for more than 60 years. To supply his summer guests with the best and freshest food, in 1865, Thompson bought and ran a very large farm in Leonardo located along today's Thompson Avenue and stretching from Route 36 to the bay shore. After the Civil War, to accommodate the great influx of visitors to Highlands, the Thompson Pavilion was expanded with perhaps two annexes, increasing capacity to some 500 guests.

The Thompson Pavilion was one of the premier hotels and one of the best-known and best-loved resorts along the Jersey shore during the nineteenth century. The hotel register, which survived as late as 1920, often displayed in a shop window in Atlantic Highlands, contained the names of notable personalities of the age, such as Charles Dana of the *Sun*, Horace Greeley of the *Tribune*, and James Bennett of the *Herald* and dated 1857, James Buchanan, President of the United States, as well as Robert Todd Lincoln, the only son of President Lincoln to reach adulthood. Men like these, prominent newspaper publishers and leaders of the nation, did for Highlands much what President U.S. Grant later would do by his summer visiting for Long Branch, making it an extremely desirable seasonal watering place, not so much for society's elite, but for upper middle class and common man elements of the city communities to the north. The popular magazine press referred to it in typically florid terms as "that romantic and pleasant summer resort . . . so beautifully located on the Highlands," thus increasing the appeal for tourists.

In April 1899, after Joseph Thompson's death, his properties were sold at auction attracting potential buyers from as far away as New York. The farm was sold for $19,350. Thompson's son-in-law, John Riker, bought the hotel for $26, 275. He eased his brother-in-law, John I. Thompson, from its management and operated the business himself successfully for more than a dozen years. Thompson's Atlantic Pavilion, the old Thompson House, was torn down on October 13, 1915, and the property was laid out in building lots. Today, all that is left of the hotel are postcards, magazine reports, and two street names, Thompson and Riker Streets, running off Portland Road, in Highlands.

On June 13, 1854, Ann F. Jarvis, a resident of New York City, purchased almost 6 acres from Maria Jarvis, who had bought the land from Mr. and Mrs. Peter F. Schenck on December 27, 1852. The acreage was located along the river close to the new steamboat dock situated in front of Thompson's, where she had a New York builder named William S. Polhemus construct a three-story hotel (with servants' quarters on the fourth or attic floor), designed by city architect Andrew B. Taft. It was an elaborate building accommodating 126 guests with a piazza on the property near the dock and cost the huge sum of $7,578, including furnishings. This was named the Sea View House and stood between Thompson's Pavilion and Schenck's Hotel, now expanded and called Schenck's Pavilion. Miss Jarvis and perhaps her sister-in-law, Maria, had cottages near the hotel. She leased the hotel operation to various managers, specifically to William W. Smith and the bar operation to a David C. Lent in 1857.

The Sea View House was the scene of the notorious murder of Albert S. Moses on August 1, 1857, by James P. Donnelly. This was unfortunate for both Moses, who was stabbed to death, and Donnelly, who was hanged for the murder despite his apparent innocence. However, it proved fortunate for history, for the trial testimony revealed many fascinating details about summer hotel operations along the shore during that period. The incident proved beneficial to Highlands as well in so far as the publicity the murder and trial generated in the local and city press brought further attention to the summer hotels at the Highlands.

At the time of the trial, Schenck's Pavilion included the main hotel for guests, a barbershop, a bowling alley, a bar, and stables and probably Schenck's home in mostly separate buildings. The Sea View House was totally destroyed by fire, perhaps an arson committed by the Irish servants, sometime about 1864, when generally the hotel and tourist trade all over the shore were in a recession due to the Civil War.

In the decade prior to the Civil War, a period of expanded development and tourism, the resident population of Highlands more than doubled and a large part of this increase can be attributed to the influx of American-born persons from New York (26 persons) and Irish (34) and German (6) immigrants. From the long litany of Irish names, three stand out as arch-typical Highlands Irish names: Fay, McGarry, and Horan. These Irish families, who arrived during this first period of immigration, usually maintained themselves apart from the rest of the residents, an immigrant minority as opposed to the longtime American majority; Catholics as opposed to Methodist or Reformed Protestants; farm workers or general laborers as opposed to clammers or watermen. They settled in the hillsides of upper Highlands rather than in Parkertown in lower Highlands. They appear to have been as well educated and supportive of schooling for their children as the rest of the people in Highlands at this time.

The Irish listed in the 1860 U.S. Census register may first have come to Highlands as hotel workers. The staff of the Sea View House, site of the infamous 1857 Donnelly

James McGarry was an Irish immigrant who worked for the Hartshornes and was an influential leader of the town's nineteenth-century Irish Catholics. Seen here, McGarry's house (constructed in 1856 and the second oldest in town) was used as a center for Catholic services until a chapel was leased in 1877 and a church built in 1887.

murder, were Irish immigrants according to the trial testimony. The fire that destroyed the large hotel in the 1860s was suspected to have been arson, committed by the Irish servants in retaliation for the execution of Donnelly. These, like probably all the Irish in Highlands at this time, derived from the poor Irish neighborhoods of New York, coming away looking for work. Others like the McGarries and Horans no doubt also came through New York to Highlands to take work and housing with the Hartshornes, who, according to the census registers, always employed, directly or through their supervisor known as Squire Van Kirk, a fair number of Irish. John Horan, the progenitor of most all the Horans in Highlands through the years and still today, first appears as a Hartshorne farm laborer. Bridgit Horan, a sister or cousin, was a household worker or maid.

James McGarry, like his relatives Timothy and Barkley, was a Hartshorne employee for many years; he later set out on his own, but always maintained a respect for and relationship with all the Hartshornes. To McGarry's credit, he was able to build his own home in 1856 on the lot where it still stands today, slightly enlarged, but much the same as when he and his large family resided there. McGarry was something of a leader of the local immigrant Irish Catholics, and it was in his little house that the first Mass was celebrated in Highlands. The priest would come like an old-time missionary on horseback or on the steamboat from New York and especially from Red Bank on an irregular basis. McGarry would host the priest overnight before a Sunday Mass, and upon his departure, would safely store away the Mass cups, plates, and linens, with the wine and water, in a cupboard built into the chimney, until the next time. Jennifer and George Roberts are the present owners of the old McGarry house at 179 Navesink Avenue, Highlands' second oldest residence remaining.

During the period just prior to the Civil War, all the Highlands hotels accommodated some 1,400 visitors any day of the summer. The beauty and attractions of the Highlands were recounted by vacationers returning to their homes and businesses in the city, and word-of-mouth advertising made the Highlands an increasingly more desirable destination.

The Monmouth Steamboat Company was incorporated in February 1830 with an initial capital of $20,000 by Martin Chandler, Thomas L. Parker, Peter W. Schenck, Joseph King, and Jeremiah Chandler. The company built and ran the *Saratoga*, with Joseph King as captain, operating between New York City, Sandy Hook, and Highlands. The boat ran for several years, stopping at a dock at the foot of the "government road" just about south of where Bahrs' Restaurant is located today.

It should be noted that the line was inaugurated specifically to connect the Highlands with the New York City markets and population just 26 miles and a 120-minute boat trip away. Thus, it brought goods, services, and visiting tourists to the Highlands, a spot well known to the city, as the area had been a critical focal point in the city news during the two wars with England.

Peter W. Schenck was the first developer to link his town and its economic interests by steamboat to New York; after him came Thomas H. Leonard in Atlantic Highlands and William Gelhaus in Keansburg.

Although many articles dealing with Highlands history claim the *Saratoga* as the first steamboat to stop at the Highlands, it appears the *Saratoga* was the first vessel to stop *only* at Highlands in its run from New York. According to an advertisement in the *New York Post* on June 30, 1819, it would appear that the *Franklin* was the very first steamboat to stop at the Highlands, 11 years earlier in 1819, in its run from New York to Red Bank. The ship ran only two seasons, 1819 and 1820. The 1819 article stated the following: "The new

The 187-foot-long Sea Bird, *of the Merchants Steamboat Company, operated the New York to Highlands route from 1866 to 1926.*

Steam Boat *Franklin*, Capt. B. Macey, will commence running on Thursday next for Shrewsbury; will leave Whitehall slip on Thursday, Saturday, and Tuesday at 10 o'clock a.m. and will leave Shrewsbury on Friday, Monday and Wednesday, at the same hour."

Joseph I. Thompson, founder of Thompson's Atlantic Pavilion in 1851 on the Shrewsbury south of today's bridge, appreciated Highlands as a popular visitor destination and saw the great need for tourist accommodations in Highlands during his encounters with visitors coming to town and wanting to experience the vista from and the operation of the famous Twin Lights, where he was keeper for six years.

Thompson himself got into the steamboat business after purchasing the little 56-foot *Theodore Stewart*, built in Keyport in 1868, in order to bring vacationers to his hotel. He ran her between August 1870 and May 1882, bringing visitors from a dock at Highlands station, across the river, on the New Jersey Southern Railroad line between Long Branch and the great steamboat dock in Sandy Hook for New York passengers. The little steamer also profited Thompson, for when old Monmouth Race Track opened in July 1870, the *Stewart* collected race enthusiasts from along the Raritan Bay shore and brought them to Highlands and then across to Highland station, where they boarded the trains already loaded with thousands of passengers heading to the track.

Steamboat to the Shore, by George H. Moss Jr., provides information to document a gradual increase in steamboat traffic from New York City to the Highlands area from 1819 until a peak of five to seven boats daily in the late 1850s, just prior to the Civil War. The increase in water traffic is a reliable indicator of the gradual but steady and significant economic growth the Highlands (and other bay and river towns) was beginning to experience in the first half of the century.

Just as the sailing packet boats were primarily used to haul Monmouth County produce to the city markets and only secondarily took passengers, initially the steamboats did the same. One pioneer of steamboating the Red Bank–Highlands–New York route was the industrialist James P. Allaire. He owned a New York City foundry supplied by iron ore mined and processed in the Howell Works, today called Allaire State Park. After initially using sail packet boats from Oceanport and Red Bank in the 1820s, he bought the steamboat *Bellona* in 1831 and added six other boats, the last of which was the *Orus*, making her final run in 1850. The soft coal and iron ore discovered in western Pennsylvania ended Allaire's business in 1846 and later his steamboats to New York and Highlands, but not before others were ready to jump into the lucrative freight and passenger transportation business.

During the 1850s, a maximum in steamboat traffic was reached in mid-decade when there was a competition between two boat companies for the lucrative passenger and freight traffic from the stops between Red Bank and Highlands onward to New York. The result was a price war in which each of the companies tried to undercut the other, until the price reached 6¢ per passenger for a trip from Red Bank to New York. The Red Bank Steamboat Company was started on February 19, 1852, under Captain Anthony Haggerty, and one week later, the Middletown and Shrewsbury Transportation Company was chartered under Charles G. Allen, also of Red Bank, with Captain Henry B. Parker and pilot Francis A. Little. The end result of the battle was not satisfactory either for the companies—they both went broke—or for the residents of the towns on the routes.

In the opinion of Eleanor Thompson, daughter of the owner of the Thompson Pavilion, the cheap fare brought to Highlands a "very promiscuous lot of visitors who were not always desirable." The rate war was over by 1859 or 1860 and "we [in Highlands] were relieved of this influx of objectionable visitors." She meant immigrant city people and probably poor Irish city people, some of whom were just beginning to settle in Highlands at this time. The usual rate in the 1850s was 25¢ at a time when most workmen earned much less than $1.00 per day.

A new kind of summer tourist accommodation, the private club drew New York gentlemen and their families to Highlands to enjoy the well-known attractions of the area, and the club's members, in turn, publicized these same attractions to other city dwellers, thereby increasing the desirability of tourism in and around Highlands.

The first of the three clubs to make their headquarters in the Highlands during the nineteenth century was the famous Neptune Club, organized in 1847 and incorporated in 1850. The 1858 clubhouse was described as "commodious," which is born out by a contemporary painting of the building situated in a remote and wooded spot on the Benjamin M. Hartshorne property on the north shore of the Navesink or North Shrewsbury River. It provided sheltered docking for both sailing and steam vessels belonging to the club or its members and guests, generally prominent people either socially or politically. The group had not been active since about 1900 and on February 16, 1910, the building burned to the ground.

Every novel James Fenimore Cooper brought out was avidly devoured by adventure-hungry readers who could not get enough of his stories. Cooper's *The Water Witch, the Skimmer of the Seas* not only thrilled his readers, but brought them right into the Highlands, its waters, coves, and hills. No publicist could have done better for the Highlands than Cooper.

James Fenimore Cooper (1789–1851) was a premier American author of 26 novels from 1820 to 1850. He was the son of William Cooper, founder of Cooperstown, New York, the home of baseball's Hall of Fame.

His fame as a writer rests today with his highly acclaimed and widely read "Leather-stocking Tales," such as *The Last of the Mohicans* and *The Deerslayer*. Formerly his sea tales enjoyed equal appeal with readers and critics alike. Novelists Herman Melville (*Moby Dick*) and Joseph Conrad (*Before the Mast*) admired and emulated Cooper's *The Red Rover* and *The Sea Lions*, where he crafted the sea not simply as the setting, but as a principal character in a moral drama.

Cooper wrote *The Water Witch* in 1830 living with his family in Sorrento, Italy, in a villa overlooking the bay and sea, much like the villa in *The Water Witch* overlooking the bay, the Hook, and the ocean. He worked from notes, sketches, memories from his time at sea, and in his experiences of patrol work in the New York City local waters in 1805 to 1811. He had memorized the scenery and geography of the area, the New York Harbor, Raritan and Sandy Hook Bays, the Shrewsbury River and inlet from the sea, and the hills and bluffs of the Highlands.

The principal events in the tale are dominated by the Skimmer of the Seas, a figure inspired by the legends of Robert William Kidd, or Captain Kidd the Pirate, the infamous privateer turned pirate and scourge of British shipping. The time is 1720, some 20 years after Kidd's death, and the Skimmer deals in illicit trade, in untaxed and stolen goods. This brings him to do business with the supposedly respectable Jersey gentleman named Alderman Van Beverout, whose summer villa called "Lust in Rust" hangs on the west bank of the Shrewsbury River in the Highlands. This residence is none other than the old Nimrod Woodward hotel of Revolutionary times. Here, he becomes taken by the gentleman's niece, the lovely Alida, the lady La Barberie. But there is a rival, Captain Cornelius Van Cuyler Ludlow of Her Majesty's cruiser *Coquette* in pursuit of the Skimmer.

However, the inspiration for the residence "Lust for Rust" has a very interesting local legend attached to it. While Cooper was composing his novel in 1830, the place was bought by a Mrs. Stewart of New York City; she set up her son, a physician, in the house, perhaps as a gift for his soon-to-be marriage.

After Dr. Stewart left college, he fell in love with a beautiful young lady and became engaged to marry her. Unfortunately, she was stricken down with some disease and died. This so overwhelmed his nature that the world and society had no further charm for him. He hid himself in this lonely retreat and brooded over his irreparable loss. Living totally alone, he wandered and was frequently seen carrying an anatomical skeleton, which he seemed to believe was the image of his lost love. Death came soon, leaving only a surviving brother and sister by whom his effects were sold. A local physician bought the skeleton he had so long cherished, and upon examining the bones, there was found stuffed into the eye sockets and interstices of the skull a large amount in bank notes, which he returned to the family.

When Frank Leslie produced his first *Illustrated Newspaper* in 1855, he created a revolution in the business of journalism by using wood engravings to print true-to-life images of people, places, and events around which he crafted attention-grabbing feature and news articles, even injecting a bit of sensationalism and earthy realism into the media. Leslie's technological innovation was the preparation of a large detailed engraving by dividing it into column-wide sections to be engraved simultaneously by a team of artists.

Barber and Howe's Historical Collections *of 1844 shows the 1828 light towers plus a temporary substitute light tower and suggests triplet lights.*

Generally speaking, prior to this time, the production of engraved books took many weeks of work in wood or steel, and newspapers were rather routine, unimaginative, sheets of columns of words. Even monthly magazines, while having better layouts, still generally lacked images, except those generated by the writers in the minds of the readers. Leslie actually tapped into the current and longstanding American fascination with photographic images (ambrotypes, tintypes, cartes de visites, and stereographs of exotic places), which at the time could not be reproduced in print except as engravings.

In just a short time, *Frank Leslie's Illustrated Newspaper* was annually selling 500,000 copies throughout the United States at 10¢ each. Other illustrated newspapers, magazines, and books followed Leslie's lead, titles such as *Frank Leslie's Popular Monthly, Harper's Weekly* (100,000 circulation in 1865), *Harper's Monthly Magazine, Harper's New Monthly Magazine, Appleton's Journal, Balou's Pictorial Drawing-Room Companion,* and a "coffee table book" *Picturesque America.*

It is not an exaggeration to say that *Leslie's* and *Harper's* covered every topic imaginable throughout the world in images and words. Highlands was featured in several issues of these publications over the years, focusing popular attention on the town and nearby area and convincing the city readers of the desirability of Highlands as a tourist destination. One of the earliest examples of Highlands in the media was in the following *Frank Leslie's Illustrated Newspaper* of August 22, 1857:

> Being thoroughly wearied of the furnace-like atmosphere and burning streets of this modern Gotham, we determined to set out on a pilgrimage in search of some cool spot. . . . Safely embarked on board the enterprising little steamer *Alice Price,* it was but a short distance before we were . . . en route for Long Branch. . . . We were surprised to see the boat so full . . but the captain . . . told us that the Long Branch boats were always crowded. . . . In the Lower Bay we crossed to Sandy Hook and entered the Shrewsbury River here separated from the ocean by the long stretch or bar of land of which Sandy Hook forms the extreme point. . . . The salt breezes, wafted across the bar, blew off gentlemen's hats, set ladies' mantles fluttering and showed not the smallest respect to rank, age or sex. . . .

Up the Shrewsbury river to the first steamboat landing, at the Highlands of Nevesink, was a short and pleasant progress, but soon after we ran aground, and came to a dead stop, much to our discomfiture. However, the captain told us that . . . all we had to do was to wait patiently until the tide should think proper to help us out of our dilemma again. . . .

The Highlands of Nevesink are extremely romantic and as we glided along a panoramic succession of lovely views met our eyes, such as are witnessed in few other localities. The fine light-houses at a short distance from the beach, the cottages scattered along the shores, and the long line of purple woods, which we could just distinguish along the background in the evening twilight, which was beginning to close around the scene, gave a life and animation to the whole picture, which was all it needed to be one of the finest prospects in the United States.

In this neighborhood we passed a fine hotel, called the Sea View House, and the name is singularly appropriate, for it commands a magnificent aspect of the sea, over the narrow neck of land on the other side of Shrewsbury River.

This beautiful situation possesses many attractions—excellent fishing, fine sea-bathing, and capital accommodations. It is of easy access, being only two hours from New York (the fare is but twenty-five cents), and is, consequently, much frequented by New Yorkers. . . .

When the reports of war first exploded across the headlines of the New York newspapers, detailing the rebellion's beginnings at Fort Sumter in secessionist South Carolina on April 12, 1861, one can only speculate about how the news was received by

This steel engraving by Granville Perkins appeared in the 1872 publication Picturesque America. *As can be seen in this romantic view, Highlands was a popular tourist destination.*

the people in Highlands. No letters, diaries, and news or magazine reports of Highlands veterans or families have survived, if indeed any were written, to provide today's generations information on their emotions, thoughts, and actions during these troubling times. Newspaper reports dealing with the war covered other places, such as Matawan, Middletown, and Freehold, deemed more important than Highlands. One then is left to make suppositions based on the official information available.

Steamboat connections between Highlands and New York were drastically reduced, but apparently never cut completely in order to keep local produce in the city markets, mainly because the boats were pressed into military service for the duration of the war. Three boats owned by Stacy Pitcher, the *Highland Light*, the *Meta*, and the *Helen*, were leased to the government. The new 181-foot *River Queen*, built in Keyport in 1864, immediately was leased to the War Department to serve as the dispatch boat of General Grant. The vessel became even more historically important when it was used for a meeting of General Ulysses S. Grant, General William T. Sherman, Admiral David Porter, and President Abraham Lincoln to discuss peace options. The scene was captured on canvass by G.P.A. Healy and entitled *The Peacemakers*. After the war, in 1867, this boat was used in the New York to Sandy Hook connection for the Long Branch and Sea Shore Railroad Company.

The traffic level during the war was almost the same as that of the early days in the 1830s, suggesting a significant reduction in the number of passengers traveling to Highlands and similar towns compared to the large volume in the decade before the war. Being uneasy about the war, people stayed at home, were left alone with their husbands,

Seen here in an 1861 Harper's Weekly *engraving, the 10th Regiment New York Volunteers were dispatched to Sandy Hook in anticipation of a Confederate attack on the approaches to New York City.*

sons, and friends far away in the army or navy, suffered high inflation as it ate away at earnings and savings, harbored fear from the possibility that Confederate ships might assault New York, and endured political disturbances and even rioting over the conduct of the war.

Shortly after the start of the war, a half regiment of soldiers was stationed at Sandy Hook, where they probably used the barracks previously built for the laborers working on the construction of the fort there. *Harper's Weekly* of June 22, 1861, shows a picture of these men, the 10th Regiment New York Volunteers, quartered in two-story barracks and arrayed in their glamorous uniforms of the National Zouaves. What a stir the soldiers in their flashy red pantaloons and exotic fez caps must have made when on leave in Highlands, capturing the attention of the young men as potential recruits and the hearts of the young women and girls, modeled as they were after the French-Algerian crack drill team that thrilled the nation the year before. The unit was swiftly removed, being needed more urgently in Virginia than at Sandy Hook, after the Union defeat on July 21, 1861, at Bull Run, the sobering battle that warned the North that the war would be long and bloody.

Other military and civilian personnel employed on the fort at Sandy Hook lived in Highlands and commuted to work each day on Captain Josiah Lamplew's boat. Lieutenant Thompson, who was "in charge of the Ft. on Sandy Hook," according to the 1860 Census, and mechanics John Judson and George S. Welsh were boarders in town with the Lamplew family. From April 1863 through July 1866, there was stationed on Sandy Hook a minimum of one company, 750 to 1,000 men and officers, of infantry or artillery troops. From this time through the permanent deactivation of Fort Hancock on December 31, 1974, these soldiers, in typical army fashion, sought recreation in the attractions of the nearest town of Highlands. While their presence certainly helped the town's economy, from the start, it also caused residents and business owners problems, such as domestic disputes, fighting, drunkenness, and breach of the peace.

Of greatest concern was the welfare of the 20 boys Highlands families wished a safe and speedy return. The following are the names of the Highlands boys (with company, regiment, and occupation) in the Civil War:

> Elias Atwater, Co. D 29 New Jersey Volunteers (NJV), fisherman
> Matthew Brown, Co. D 29 NJV, farm laborer
> George B. Davis, Navy, farm laborer
> Joseph Eldridge, Navy, waterman (or clammer)
> Albert Havens, civilian telegrapher in Signal Corps
> George W. Lewis, Co. D 29 NJV, waterman
> Robert H. Lewis, Co. D 29 NJV, waterman
> David Matthews, Co. D 29 NJV and Co. A 38 NJV (1864), waterman
> George W. Marks, Co. D 29 NJV, farm laborer
> John C. Mount, Co. F 29 NJV, waterman
> Horatio Mount, Co. F New York Mounted Rifles, farm laborer
> Charles H. Parker, Co. D 29 NJV, waterman
> George W. Parker, Co. G 32 Massachusetts Volunteers, waterman

Jacob H. Parker, Co. A 38 NJV (1864) corporal, waterman

Lewis M. Parker, Co. D 29 NJV and Co. A 38 NJV (1864, as corporal), waterman

William F. Parker, Co. G 32 Massachusetts Volunteers, waterman

William P. Smith, unit not known

Horatio Tilton, Co. D. 29 NJV, farm laborer

William H. Van Dyke, Co. F NJV and Co. A 38 NJV (as wagoner), waterman

Edgar B. Welch, Co. D 29 NJV.

This amounts to a total of 20 enlistments. However, three men served two enlistments: David Matthews, George W. Lewis, and William Van Dyke. Irishman Edgar Welch did not have to serve at all, being a resident alien at the time. Highlands resident Peter F. Schenck, grandson of the noted soldier in the Revolutionary War, in 1864 received a $200 bonus to enlist in the 38 New Jersey Volunteers, but he instead bought a substitute, Hugh Rock, to take his place (perfectly legal at the time, yet strongly opposed especially by poor Irish and German immigrants in the cities). The number of enlistments is rather remarkable, for this represents 20 men out of a total Highlands population of 213 persons.

The reasons that led so many men to join were no doubt complex and different for each man. However, in general, they joined out of a sense of duty to preserve the Union and to punish the secessionist rebels. They joined because they were swept up in the glory of the cause and the excitement of the game of war. They joined because family and friends were going to war: brothers John and Horatio Mount; brothers George and Robert Lewis; brothers Charles, George, Jacob, Lewis, and William Parker. All the Highlands men were friends or acquaintances in so small a town. They joined to avoid the draft set to begin September 3, 1862, and because they believed the nine-month soldiers would not see combat. They joined for the economic advantage army service brought them and their families.

It is instructive to see what army service paid a Highlands man, David Matthews, for example. David Matthews, a private in Company D 29 New Jersey Volunteers, served nine months, from September 1862 to June 1863, for $117, plus a total of $54 dependent bounty collected by his wife each month at Town Hall. In Matthews's second enlistment as a private in Company A 38 New Jersey Volunteers, he served nine months, September 6, 1864, through June 30, 1865, for $144, plus $54 dependent bounty, plus $400 re-enlistment bounty, for a total of $598.

When this soldier's pay is compared to a civilian's pay, especially to a clammer's pay, one begins to appreciate the big turnout from Highlands. In 1860, a young man starting in an office or business and who could read, write, and count would receive $150 per year. A farm laborer would be paid about $135 to $150 per year, while a male teacher after the war was paid $375 for nine months. A clammer's annual pay may have been about $150 to $185 per year, which included the labor of the clammer's wife as well.

The financial advantage always had to be weighed against the possibility of being killed or seriously wounded in action, of being taken prisoner, becoming seriously ill, or even dying from disease. Fortunately, none of the Highlands soldiers or sailors were killed or wounded, and in the whole 29th Regiment, only one man from Keyport died due to combat wounds. However, John C. Mount was discharged early from the U.S. Army

Hospital in Washington on May 7, 1863, due to "disability." One lad named Edward T. Burdge returned to Riceville / Navesink from mustering in at Camp Vredenburg in Freehold and died of typhoid, which he and so many soldiers contracted from the unsanitary living conditions and from exposure to the ills of thousands of men from all over the North. This was a time when most Highlands men had never been out of town or in a crowd of strangers.

Civil War veterans and relatives played significant roles in Highlands history. George Eldridge, while his son Joseph was in the war, invented the hard clam rake, which practically revolutionized the clamming industry, increasing annual harvests and income. Albert Havens and his brothers Vinton and Arthur were expert telegraphers, following in the footsteps of their father, Charles. Arthur was the first telegrapher at the CNJ Railroad station in Atlantic Highlands.

George W. Lewis served as assistant keeper at the Twin Lights, leaving as first assistant keeper in July 1879 to soon build the Lewis House (131 Navesink Avenue) hotel to meet the needs of a great tourist influx into Highlands in the 1880s. His daughter, Jennie, married Demarest T. Herbert, who built and developed much of Highlands, and their daughter, Beatrice, married Fred Bedle of the Bedle Drug Store, the father of Katharine Bedle Bohinski James. Robert Lewis worked on the steamboats stopping at Highlands from 1865 through 1900 and was captain of the Patten Line's *Elberon*.

John C. Mount's son, Richard, became one of the Borough of Highlands' first councilmen in 1900. Charles H. Parker was a religious man who, as deacon and incorporator, started the first church in Highlands, the Reformed Church in 1875. Lewis Parker, like his brother, was an elder of the Reformed Church from its start. His son, Abram, was the first Borough of Highlands tax assessor in 1900. His daughter, Louella,

Civil War veterans of the 29th Regiment of New Jersey Volunteers held their annual "encampment" at the Baptist church in Atlantic Highlands in 1894.

became an early-1900s schoolteacher in town and later married Dr. John Opfermann. After the war, George W. Parker hosted Methodist classes in his home with the Reverend Robert Emery from Atlantic Highlands and helped build the first Methodist Episcopal church in 1886. His son, Reuben, was elected to commissioner of appeals in the first government of the Borough of Highlands in 1900.

A service summary of the 29th Regiment New Jersey Volunteers reveals how very fortunate the Highlands men were in the war. The regiment was organized, officered, equipped, and mustered into United States service by September 20, 1862. After eight days of drill, the green recruits shipped out by train for the defense of Washington, D.C. completing two forts and standing guard duty on the Harper's Ferry Road. On November 30, it marched 80 miles down the Potomac to be taken by steamboat to Acquia Creek, where it guarded the vital railroad supply link to Fredericksburg. Caught in a two-day December snowstorm without shelter and rations, the men suffered from widespread illness but continued guard duty until four companies, including D and F (where the Highlands men were), were sent December 11 to the supply depot at Falmouth on the Rappahannock River, opposite rebel-held Fredericksburg, about to be stormed by Union artillery and troops. The Highlands men helped guard the pontoon bridges during the crossings and then were ordered for three days to patrol the streets of Fredericksburg looking for Confederate snipers, Union deserters, and preventing looting of homes by Union soldiers. The battle of Fredericksburg was a disastrous Union defeat with heavy casualties, resulting in the whole army's retreat back across the river under fierce Confederate cannonade. The Highlands men and comrades in the 29th Regiment were the last to cross, all safely.

The regiment continued guard duty of the railroad through Christmas and New Year's Day until January 10, 1863, when it joined the First Corps of the Army of the Potomac. The men expected action with the enemy but received only long days of drill, until the whole army started the infamous five-day "Mud March," another fiasco of General Burnside, wherein the men suffered badly in Virginia's winter of wet and cold with roads of mud 18 inches deep. Burnside, soon to be replaced by General Hooker, called off the maneuver January 24, a happy day for the men who were told that they would get their first pay since mustering into service. Lincoln's Emancipation Proclamation was not well received by most of the regiment, and there were grumblings, "It will prove more disastrous than the camp fever to the soldiers . . . Complaints . . . nothing but 'nigger' for the remedy . . . Can't 'nigger' the army a great deal longer." Throughout February, March, and most of April, General Hooker improved morale with better living conditions and leaves, keeping the men in winter camp engaged in exercises and drills to prepare for a spring offensive, the battle of Chancellorsville.

Hooker's main army crossed the Rappahannock above Fredericksburg while the First Division, with the Highlands men, crossed to create a diversion south of the city, April 30. When Hooker's main army was outmaneuvered by Lee's genius tactics and began to be overrun on May 2, the First Division quickly re-crossed the river to make a forced march up to support the main Union force. Confederate cannons caught the men of the 29th at the river with two bursts, mortally wounding Corporal Devoe, causing Private Thomas Compton to lose a foot in surgery, and hospitalizing two others with serious wounds.

The original towers were deteriorating so badly that they had to be replaced by the present structure in 1862.

None of the Highlands men was hurt. The First Corps' presence south of the river proved useless to Hooker, for his battle was already lost.

On June 12, they were on the march north following Lee's army intent on invading Pennsylvania, stopping to witness the execution of a man from the 19th Indiana for desertion, and proceeding on until June 16, when the men got the happy orders to leave the First Corps and return to New Jersey. The men reached Freehold on June 18 and were mustered out at Camp Vredenburg on June 28 and returned home. A week later news reached Highlands telling of the tragic fate of the men in their old First Corps in the Battle of Gettysburg.

In Highlands, during the war, Federal officers turned their attention to the improvement of the Twin Lights. Compared to the earlier construction and renovation of the Twin Lights, much more work was needed to construct the 1861–1862 (or present) Twin Lights structure, requiring many laborers at a time when it was extremely difficult or practically impossible to get experienced stone workers and general laborers to travel from the city. Because mechanics and laborers refused to travel just to get work, many private, city, and U.S. government projects offered work right at home and at great pay rates during the Civil War years. However, Highlands men and other local laborers no doubt contributed much to the success and speed of the construction, in much the same way they were hired for work there during the time when their employment was documented in the local newspapers.

First, the octagonal north tower was constructed, followed by the square south tower. The two were then connected by the 18-room living quarters of keeper Gordon Sickles and his family and his two assistant keepers, John Garrity and Peter Herbert (and their families, although they may likely have been single men). The material used was brick-lined gray freestone imported from Bellville, New Jersey. After this, the old 1828 towers had to be torn down and all the stones removed from the site. The total cost of construction was $47,000.

Both towers had first-order, white, fixed lights of 8,000 candle power fueled by lard oil, and the south tower still had its Fresnel lens, making the Twin Lights the brightest in the United States at the time.

Where all the stones and soil excavated for the new building were taken or dumped is one of the mysteries of the Twin Lights. Keeper Gordon B. Sickles, last keeper of the old and first keeper of the new Twin Lights, saw it all but took the information to his grave. Recently, some light was shed on this in June 1999, when Monmouth University professor Richard Veit led a group of students in an excavation of the 1828 tower sites. They discovered that the tower foundations were still there below the ground just a couple of feet, revealing that only the above-ground portion of the towers had been torn down.

Soon, remarkable changes were made to the lights, for in 1883, mineral oil replaced lard oil in the north tower, a U.S. first, to produce 10,000 candle power. Then, in 1898, the hill burst with a brilliance of 25,000,000 candle power created by an arc lamp inside a French-designed bivalve lens in the south tower, fed with electricity from an oil-fired steam generator in an adjacent out-building. The north tower light was extinguished and kept in reserve for emergencies. The new powerful single light at the Twin Lights flashed a 1/10 second signal every 5 seconds, visible directly 22 miles and from cloud illumination some 70 miles at sea.

During the previously mentioned Professor Veit's archaeological excavation of the old 1828 sites, the students found smoking pipe fragments and oyster shells and suggested these were likely left by the many tourists who continually came to Highlands and its Twin Lights grounds to enjoy the breezes, the views, and picnic lunches, something still done by tourists today. The existence of the pipes and shell fragments, even without further interpretive information, suggests very frequent visitation by the public during the period of the earlier towers, from 1828 through 1862.

This attraction for tourists is well documented by early illustrations in *Frank Leslie's Illustrated Newspaper* depicting the light towers, the extensive vistas of Highlands below, Sandy Hook, and the ocean dotted with ships out to the horizon, and the many ladies, gentlemen and children in groups enjoying the site. An article from the *Red Bank Register* (July 20, 1910) also mentions the attraction:

> This year as they have for the last 50 years or more, The Twin Lights on the hill are a great attraction. Almost every day the lights are visited and the lighthouse tender delights in taking the new comer up the tower into the revolving lamp where they have a fine view of the ocean and the surrounding country for miles. In the rear of the lighthouse is a large stretch of open ground for basket parties and during the past week over 500 persons have eaten their lunches there.

Another major construction project considered vitally import at the time to involve Highlands workmen was the fort at Sandy Hook. Although the strategic advantage to New York City of Sandy Hook had been known from American experiences during the Revolutionary War and the War of 1812, when a wooden artillery fortress had been hastily constructed there, the first effort to construct a real fort was made only in 1851 in a report to Congress. In 1858, preliminary work was started with the building of a dock and pier on the bay side and offices, warehouses, barracks, and mess halls for the resident workmen.

It was to be a pentagon-shaped massive granite block masonry fort of titanic proportions, with three sides housing cannons facing the sea and two sides facing the land with defensive gun ports. Work progressed according to schedule when the Civil War broke out in April 1861, and the worry of Confederate warships focused the effort on preparing the sea-facing walls to receive their 8- and 10-inch guns (installed in 1863).

Considerable delays throughout the years 1862–1864 were caused by shortages of materials and their delivery and of urban mechanics and laborers who refused to work at Sandy Hook, preferring the better wages and conveniences of work nearer home. This benefited the Highlands men and other local fishermen and farm laborers financially just as did the construction at the Twin Lights, providing incomes two to three times higher than clamming, fishing, or farm work.

Shortly after the end of the war, in 1865, all work was stopped in order to redesign the fort to make use of the technological lessons learned during the Civil War, when masonry forts like the one at Sandy Hook were pulverized by the new heavy rifled guns. The revolution in weaponry essentially made the fort at Sandy Hook obsolete. Congress refused to appropriate any money for three more years, forcing the fort, still only about 70% completed, to close down in July 1869.

Today, one of the bastions of the fort survives, serving as the foundation of a water tower in the Coast Guard area. Some of the granite was used in other construction projects in early Fort Hancock, with the rest being dumped in 1897 to create a sea wall to reduce storm erosion about half a mile south of the tip of the Hook.

Part of the bastion of the never completed fort at Sandy Hook of the Civil War era remains today supporting a Fort Hancock water reservoir.

5. The Later Nineteenth Century

In the decades following the Civil War, a community began to build in Highlands. Three churches were established, along with a true public school and a post office. More and grander homes were built, hotels were expanded, and a fire department was formed to protect the town. Actors, poets, artists, and tourists of every description came to visit or to reside, all drawn by the beauty of the place, so very close to New York via the steamboats and trains. The hard-working Highlanders, mostly clammers, watched as outside forces changed their lives perhaps for the better. However, their dissatisfaction with Middletown Township's rule, of which Highlands or Seaside was just a little far off part, continued to grow.

In 1873, the Reverend Abraham W. Allen and his wife, Josephine, two-year-old son, Nathan, and niece, Elizabeth Van Allen, arrived in Highlands probably for the sake of his health, which was failing, though he was only 57 years old. He brought his family for a life near the sea with its salt air, which was thought to be beneficial in the restoration of good health.

Reverend Allen was a Congregationalist minister and took up the challenge of bringing the Christian faith to the people of Highlands, despite his illness. He began teaching the children and visiting from house to house and held services in his own or a neighboring home. Many were converted, and a church was organized with the majority of the people deciding to place themselves under the pastoral care of the Reformed Church. Its 12 members organized the church on February 9, 1875, and constructed a little church building the same year at Fifth Street and Valley Avenue in the heart of Parkertown. Reverend Allen became their pastor, living in the vicarage, and labored for the church until his death at age 68 in December 1884. He was laid to rest in the small burial ground adjacent to the church.

The parish of Our Lady of Perpetual Help (OLPH) formally began serving the people in Highlands on November 27, 1883. However, as early as 1863 and probably a year before, area Catholics, the majority being Irish immigrants, celebrated the Eucharist in the home of James McGarry at 179 Navesink Avenue. Missionary-style services were provided by priests from St. James in Red Bank, coming by horse and carriage or steamboat.

As the faithful increased in number too great for private home worship, the Hartshornes rented them the old first schoolhouse, still located at 46 Grand Tour, from

Highlands' first church was built in 1875 under Reverend Abraham Allen, pastor of a small Dutch Reformed congregation at Fifth and Valley Streets.

1877 until 1888. During this time, several priests served the faithful, with Father John J. O'Connor being the first resident priest in 1879. Pastor Father John H. Fox oversaw the construction of the first OLPH church at Navesink Avenue and Miller Street in 1888. During the pastorate of Father John J. Sweeney, the present rectory was built in 1901, with a hall erected to the rear of the church.

As early as 1863, some residents began to organize themselves in class groups to follow the Methodist church principles, meeting in private homes. Such activity increased and came to the attention of the Reverend Robert Emery in Atlantic Highlands, just 4 miles away. Tradition tells that the reverend held services and discussion groups in the kitchen of George W. Parker and other townspeople. They met in a two-room log cabin building of Fred Kieferdorf on Fifth Street under Horatio Mount, their exhorter class leader. They had to move for more space to the Alex Weaver property, which had a store and dwelling and later they met together in the Dorsett building, the site of Benjamin J. Neimark's grocery store on Miller Street. Reverend Emery continued this missionary activity until March 29, 1885, when he came to consult with Parker and others about actually starting an official Methodist Society in Highlands. On May 10 that same year, Dr. W.W. Moffett, the presiding elder of the New Brunswick District of the New Jersey Conference of the Methodist Episcopal Church, came and formally organized the First Methodist Episcopal Church of Seaside (the name given this section of Middletown Township), establishing the Reverend Robert Emery as pastor. Money was raised totaling $1,380 and the parish erected its first church building on Miller Street, dedicating it August 22, 1886.

This building served as Highlands' old post office in the late nineteenth century.

The elders would never have selected this site, of all the hundreds of sites available in town, on which to build, had they known the Central Railroad of New Jersey would in 1892 extend its tracks from Atlantic Highlands to Highland Station across the river and lay its tracks within feet of the little white church! The situation was intolerable. Sunday services could not be held with the stentorian noise and earth tremor and rumble of the steam engines pulling long trains of coaches filled with Sunday tourists. Property was in time bought on Bay Avenue where another church building was put up. The old building and lot were sold. The Reverend Thomas Huss, pastor, led the Methodist community in prayers at the cornerstone-laying ceremony on September 3, 1908. The church was dedicated July 11, 1909, with Reverend John Handley, district superintendent, and Pastor Thomas Huss conducting the services, assisted by chairman of the trustees, Charles T. Maison, who had served the Borough as its first tax collector and second mayor.

The first post office was established at Highlands in 1852 with Peter F. Schenck as the first postmaster operating out of the Schenck Hotel. It lasted only two years but was restored in 1871. During this interval, mail was received unofficially via the New York steamboats or by stage from the Keyport Post Office or other locations, such as at Hopping Station in Belford from Red Bank via the Raritan and Delaware Bay Railroad line. Sometimes letters with stamps affixed were given to a passenger or agent of one of the steamboats who upon landing at Keyport or Highlands, for example, would deliver them to the local post office for processing and eventual delivery to the addressee. Only the railroads had postal clerks aboard special cars designated postal railroad cars on which mail was sorted and processed for delivery to post offices usually located along or very near the rail lines.

In June 1871, Charles Van Berner, a German immigrant and naturalized citizen (the huckster of the 1880 Census), was the postmaster, who, according to Thomas H. Leonard, was somewhat inept at the tasks before him and depended heavily on Leonard, the assistant postmaster in the neighboring town of Leonardville. Van Berner was followed by

J. Mortimer Johnson in July 1872 until the office was discontinued on May 17, 1875. When the office was re-established on June 4, 1875, Alexander Brand became postmaster. Timothy M. Maxson followed him on April 12, 1877, and James H. Brainard Jr. took over in February 1882 and served until October 1888, when Samuel E. Leonard became postmaster.

Then came Irish immigrant and naturalized citizen Michael Rowland from January 1889 to May 1897. Rowland was the father of Dr. James Rowland and pharmacist William Rowland of Highlands, and he also ran a hotel along the river south of the bridge. Alonzo Hand came after Rowland, serving from May 1897 to July 1913 and moving from the old post office located near the auditorium (purple building) to the new quarters at 71 Bay Avenue, where the postmaster and his family lived.

When Highlands was not Highlands, but called Seaside on the official maps and records in Middletown, the people who lived here felt the community needed its own fire department to protect the growing number of hotels, businesses, and homes in town. Thus, some 35 public-spirited men organized the Seaside Fire Department on January 30, 1894. Each had a complete red, blue, and white and gold-trimmed uniform, a badge on his hat, white belt and gloves, and "Seaside No. 1" embroidered across the blouse. Their equipment was a hand-drawn manual rocker arm pumper and a hose cart.

Although a public school district existed in Highlands, a part of Middletown Township, since 1845, the first public school building did not appear until many years later. Prior to this time, Peter W. Schenck, an early landholder in the area, built a school used for private instruction from 1834 until it was abandoned in 1845.

The Seaside Fire Company No. 1 was formed on January 30, 1894, and its members are pictured here in their red, white, and blue uniforms.

Later in 1847, formal education was conducted in a room of the old Water Witch House, made famous as the setting of James Fenimore Cooper's *The Water Witch*. This hotel was owned by Colonel William Jones and was located where his daughter, Angeline, opened a school for local children. Growing enrollment prompted Jones to build a small separate building adjacent to the 200-guest hotel.

In 1866, when Gilbert Giles purchased the property, he apparently was unwilling to continue to allow use of the old Jones school. The frame school building was sold to a man named Leonard, who moved it to his property and used it as a "grape house." However, once again public-spirited individuals provided for the Highlands children, for in 1867, Mary and Edward Hartshorne built a two-room schoolhouse on their property at 46 Grand Tour, the present home of Mary and Peter McKeown.

In 1867, the first year of publicly funded education in District 12 of Middletown Township, Mary Hartshorne, whose parents built the school, taught there. The Township paid $1 rent per annum, $20 for incidentals, and some $270 for the teacher's salary. Records of this year show 138 children between 5 and 17 living in Highlands, with only 60 enrolled in school and only 15 pupils attending the whole 10 months of the school year.

After the Monmouth County School District 67 was formed in Highlands in 1877, property was purchased for $500, and the first publicly financed school was constructed for $2,000 at the northeast corner of Navesink Avenue and Miller Street on the site of today's Horizon Condominium. Soon growing enrollment required an expanded facility, and in 1884, at a cost of $2,500, it was enlarged to two stories measuring 40 by 80 feet and described as a "fine building, furnished with all modern and improved furniture."

Highlands has been a center for clamming almost since the time the local Lenape Indians first taught the Dutch traders and English settlers in Highlands of Navesink

Highlands' first public schoolhouse dates to 1867, a gift to the town leased at $1 per annum by Edward and Mary Hartshorne. When a school was built at public expense on Navesink Avenue and Miller Street in 1877, the house was used as a Catholic chapel until 1888. It is now the home of Mary and Peter McKeown at 46 Grand Tour.

Furman Parker, seen here c. 1930, had clammed in the Highlands waters all of his life.

(meaning "place of good fishing" in the Lenape language) the harvesting techniques and the food value of the clam. Some have believed that Samuel Matthews, who lived in a cave in the hills, was the first clammer to settle in the Highlands. The story may be apocryphal, but the name Matthews and clamming go back many generations in Highlands.

It is certain, however, that John Parker and his family came from Manalapan to Highlands before 1850, when it was called Seaside as part of Middletown Township, and almost immediately took up clamming to earn a living. Parker was the founding father of the section of Highlands known to locals as Parkertown (16 families and 63 persons in 1900).

The boundaries of the village were the Shrewsbury River, Cedar Street, and the open drainage ditch running parallel to and on the riverside of today's Bay Avenue and today's North Street (originally the line of the ditch draining into the river). The name derives from the great number of interrelated individuals named Parker residing there. The first and only quasi-official recognition of the name appeared in the 1880 U.S. census as the "Village of Parkertown." In 1880, Parkertown had a total of 210 persons living in 45 households. Forty-five of these persons were named Parker.

The following piece is from one of the most popular magazines of the century, *Harper's New Monthly Magazine*, typical of the kind of journalism that charmed and enticed people to leave the crowded and hot city for the enjoyment of spending a day or a week or a summer in Highlands:

> Leaving the road [Navesink Avenue] about two miles south of Mount Mitchell [Monmouth County Park System's Mt. Mitchill Scenic Overlook], we

The village of Parkertown, depicted here c. 1880 in Harper's New Monthly Magazine, *contained 210 persons and 45 households.*

clambered down a wooded declivity [Miller Street]. Before us lay a marshy plain [the Kay and Cornwell tract not to be filled and developed until 1912], gay with meadow grasses, and dotted over by bay bushes and a few gnarled, storm twisted cedars. Beyond, on the left, a rambling street [Miller Street leading to the river], lined on either side by weather-beaten cottages and old icehouses, and paved with shells, ran down to the river. These with a few cabins standing back or grouped along the shore [Fourth and Fifth Streets] and a small brown church [Reformed Church of 1875 at Fifth and Valley Streets] comprised the fishing village of Parkertown.

As we strolled through the quiet street to the beach, groups of sunburned, yellow-haired women gazed at us from the doorways, hiding themselves behind the fences, whence they peered forth cautiously. Finding we were harmless, they followed us to the beach, looking more like kelpies [a water sprite or fairy] than human beings, with their bleached locks and nut-brown faces.

We seated ourselves on some up-turned boats. Behind us were the shabby, little houses, the women, children and shells; and near us some fishing nets spread on the fence to dry. Looking up and down the beach, we saw only drowsy signs of life—a group of cows knee-deep in the water, three small boys crabbing, a bevy of ducks floating idly by, and far over head in the blue ether a fishhawk circling on lazy wing. . . .

The evening being propitious for the sport, we rowed down [from Thompson's Pavilion at the bridge] to the little village to see eel-fishing. . . . As we approached Parkertown, lo! the drowsy little hamlet of the afternoon seemed full awake; lights flashed from the windows, flitted along the beach, and flared on the river.

Before us lay anchored a fleet of boats, each with either a pole and blazing light, or a low lamp fixed to its bow, the dusky figures of the fishermen bending forward to spear the fish, or haul it in, their eager, earnest faces lighted by the yellow glare of the smoky lamps, and the wavering reflections on the dark water, presenting a wild, fantastic picture.

Over a century ago, a best-selling New Jersey guidebook spoke of Parkertown as follows:

an odd little hamlet whose population is engaged in clamming. The soul of this original community is wrapped up in clams. They are to it what the whales once were to Nantucket. Parkertown is clamming, shelling, stringing or canning clams; devouring them or dreaming of performing one or another of these acts. Clam is said to be the first word lisped by Parkertown babies.

A number of Parkertown women and girls . . . is engaged in opening and stringing clams, $40,000 worth of which is annually shipped from this queer little hamlet to New York.

The writer Gustav Kobbe goes on to relate for the first time in any publication the various methods and techniques of harvesting clams: raking, chugging, treading, and dredging. These are basically the same methods used today as in 1889, when Kobbe's *New Jersey Coast and Pines* was published.

At first, there was no bridge, for none was needed until about 1865, when large numbers of visitors began to come from New York on the Long Branch and Seashore Rail Road, which connected with steamboats that landed on Sandy Hook. James Schenck used

The Highland Lights appear in this sketch for writer Gustav Kobbe's work in 1889.

a rowed ferry and later a steam ferry to transport passengers and cargo across the river from the Hook to the Highlands.

The first Highlands bridge was opened on December 5, 1872, having been built by the Highlands Bridge Co. It was 1,452 feet long and 18 feet wide with a swing draw of 186 feet. The Hartshornes, Edward and Robert, organized the company and the financing of the $35,000 cost. It was a toll bridge, but on July 1, 1875, before it could make a profit, a heavily-laden schooner struck and wrecked the draw. It stayed inoperable and open for several years until the Navesink Bridge Co. decided it would be profitable to buy and repair the span. Hoping to avert another collision, the new company widened the draw to 194 feet and opened the second Highlands bridge on June 27, 1878.

"I cannot describe the rejoicing that came upon us when the first railroad was built on the beach at Sandy Hook," wrote Eleanor Thompson, for this marked the start of a new surge of tourism to Highlands, which ran without significant interruption for almost a century, from the close of the Civil War in 1865 through the 1960s. Ms. Thompson was referring to the route of steamboats running from Manhattan to Sandy Hook, where they connected with the trains heading to Long Branch but stopping at "Highland" Station (thus termed by the railroad authorities!), across the river from the town of Highlands.

This transportation link between New York and Long Branch, making use of U.S. government–owned land on the Sandy Hook peninsula, had actually first been proposed to the secretary of war as early as April 1856 and tentatively approved. This permitted construction of the rail line in 1863, while final permission was granted by President Lincoln on July 21, 1864, allowing the Long Branch and Sea Shore Railroad to build from Spermaceti Cove southward during the period 1863–1865. The line was completed, after much legal and official controversy, and operational by the summer of 1865. The steamboat *Neversink* made the first run from the city to Sandy Hook on July 31, 1865.

The first Highlands Bridge was constructed by the Highlands Bridge Company and opened on December 5, 1872.

During the summer months of 1865 through 1869, this route ran in direct competition with the Raritan and Delaware Bay Railroad, which had a steamboat link in Port Monmouth since 1860 connecting to Red Bank. After its business troubles compounded by the effects of the Civil War and its ultimate failure, its tourist traffic was taken by the Sandy Hook boat-trains. However, while both lines served Long Branch ultimately, only the Sandy Hook route afforded rail connections to the Highlands.

Initially, tourists from the city boarded the train at Spermaceti Cove, and later (1870) at the Horse Shoe Cove farther north on Sandy Hook, and could elect to get off at Highland Station. Here, they could take the ferry provided by James Schenck to the grand riverside hotels directly across the Shrewsbury. Later on in 1872, they could actually walk across the river, making use of the foot/carriage toll bridge located just north of the present Highlands–Sea Bright bridge. From July 1875 to June 1878, Schenck resumed his ferry service since the bridge draw, damaged by a passing schooner, was stuck open during this period.

The Long Branch and Sea Shore line became part of the New Jersey Southern Railroad in 1879, and it in turn was taken over by the Central Rail Road of New Jersey (CRRNJ) in 1882.

In 1865, when service first began, the rates were $1 for a single trip, $1.50 for a round trip excursion, and $20 for a monthly commutation. Two boats ran daily, except Sundays (the Christian Sabbath), and on Saturdays, a special excursion was provided for the early daytrippers, leaving New York at 10:30 a.m. and leaving Long Branch 6:15 p.m. with arrival in New York at 7:30 p.m. In the 1870s, six boats in service were running three trips daily, making for a total of some 18 boat trains arriving and departing. If each carried 1,000 passengers on the best days in the season, well over 18,000 tourists were hitting the attractions in Long Branch, the premier watering place of the Jersey shore and the *raison d'etre* of the steamboat-railroad connection to the city, with secondary resort towns like Sea Bright and Highlands taking perhaps 25% of the tourists and their dollars.

The Central of New Jersey by 1880 extended its line from Matawan to Keyport, where a 2,000-foot-long pier accommodated steamboats feeding the city with Monmouth County seafood and farm produce. Later in 1883, the defunct Delaware and Raritan Bay line, with its Port Monmouth pier, was bought out by a group of Atlantic Highlands businessmen headed by John Applegate of Red Bank and Thomas H. Leonard of Atlantic Highlands. From Port Monmouth, a line was constructed to Atlantic Highlands. They named it the Atlantic Highlands and New York Railroad and opened it with a grand ceremony on July 12, 1883, hoping for a deluge of tourists and potential residents coming from the city. Only a trickle of passengers used the line and caused financial disaster for the company's stockholders. It was sold on March 15, 1888, to the Central Railroad of New Jersey (CNJ) which also bought the existing steamboat pier in Atlantic Highlands on April 22, 1889, and rebuilt it to receive trains meeting the steamboats (the *Monmouth* was the first) from New York. This company then extended its line to Port Monmouth from Keyport.

For some time prior to this, the U.S. government had been pressuring the railroad to cease its steamboat-train operation on Sandy Hook, which it ultimately did, but not before extending its line from Atlantic Highlands to Highlands along the water's edge on Sandy

The tracks of the Central Railroad of New Jersey, seen here in 1892, helped in bringing thousands of tourists to Highlands in the late nineteenth century.

Hook Bay. The CNJ company then reconstructed the county's vehicle bridge, creating a wider draw common to the trains and vehicles, thus effecting an X-shaped bridge. The railroad bridge allowed connection with the railroad running through Sea Bright and Monmouth Beach to Long Branch. The railroad line and steamboat dock at Horseshoe Cove on Sandy Hook were discontinued, although the CNJ company did maintain its line in Sandlass's Highland Beach resort. The new railroad was opened on May 30, 1892.

Now for the first time, Highlands was directly on the railroad line of the Central Railroad of New Jersey. Tourists from the cities of New York, Brooklyn, Newark, and Jersey City came to Highlands either via the all-rail route from Jersey City through Matawan and along the entire bayshore or via the popular summer steamboat-train route using the boat-train pier at Atlantic Highlands, still referred to as the Sandy Hook route, although the Sandy Hook peninsula facilities were no longer used.

Long before the advent of trolleys, busses, and automobiles, horse-drawn stagecoaches met the steamboats and trains arriving from the city and carried both visitors and local residents to villages throughout the area of the Highlands. The "People's Line" ran well before the Civil War and later was purchased by Andrew Bowne. In 1867, it, in turn, was bought and managed by Charles H. Greene with the great appreciation of the residents and businessmen of the area community as late as 1907, when the Jersey Central Traction Company's trolleys started.

The original route started at Highlands and ran through Navesink, Atlantic Highlands, Leonardville, to Belford's "Hopping Station" (alias Navesink Station, located south of the intersection of Leonardville Road and Hopping Road, just a little east of Campbell's Junction) on the old train line (Raritan and Delaware Bay, later the New Jersey Southern), which ran from Red Bank to the steamboat pier in Port Monmouth from 1865 to 1869. From there, it continued to Middletown village. After Atlantic Highlands built its first long pier and steamboats landed there, Green's stage met passengers there as well. Another stage line operated by a man named Tompkins ran from Highlands to Keyport, making one round-trip daily, meeting the New York steamboat there and returning in the afternoon. Yet another competitive stage company ran from Middletown along the King's Highway to the train line and then up into Chapel Hill and down through Navesink (then called Riceville) and up along Navesink Avenue (today's Route 36) to the steamboat docks and the Shrewsbury River ferry and later bridges to the train at Highland Station.

The Central Railroad of New Jersey wanted to take advantage of the economic development of the shore, and to do so, it needed a continuous line from Matawan to Long Branch. It also was being compelled by the government to remove its ferry and rail operation from Sandy Hook by 1892. It then bought the bridge, modified it so that a common draw of 200 feet could serve trains, vehicles, and pedestrians, and opened the third Highlands bridge on May 30, 1892.

The most important industry, besides fishing, involves tourist accommodations, for which Highlands had been perhaps known best throughout most of the nineteenth century. The hotels along the river and later a bit removed from it provided the magnets that attracted and held city people in adult groups and families to come to Highlands for

This wood engraving from Appleton's Journal *of 1872 captures the excitement of Charles H. Greene's stagecoach racing down Navesink Avenue.*

just a day, a weekend, a week's vacation, or even for the entire summer season. Places like Thompson's Atlantic Pavilion were social centers providing musical and dramatic entertainments and dancing; great dining rooms serving breakfast, lunch, and dinner, especially in the form of the famous Highlands shore dinner (the seafood dinner today); drinks for respectable ladies and gentlemen at one of several bars; and rooms comfortable with windows providing ocean air and views. These luxurious hotels were conveniently located on the direct steamboat lines, on the steamboat-and-train lines, and later on the direct train lines, all bringing people escaping the city in summer with a 90-minute ride. The town offered natural and historical sites to entertain and was located within easy distance from other places, such as Red Bank, Long Branch, and the Monmouth Park races.

The fourth hotel to appear along the river was built by local carpenter James H. Giles close to the water below the site of the destroyed Sea View House, for Benjamin M. Hartshorne in 1879. Called the Pavilion Hotel, it was soon leased to Thomas Swift and became known as the Swift House. It burned to ashes in 1884 and was immediately rebuilt by Swift, now the owner.

In the mid-1880s, another hotel was constructed in Highlands, not along the river, but on the south side of Navesink Avenue a short distance to the east of Miller Street. This small hotel was built by George W. Lewis, Highlands native, Civil War veteran, and former assistant keeper at Twin Lights. This marks the first departure from development along the river for summer tourist accommodations. The hotel was later run by Jennie Lewis

The Lewis Hotel was built by Civil War veteran George W. Lewis, a carpenter and former Twin Lights assistant keeper.

and her husband, Demarest T. Herbert. The Lewis House, minus its two level porch facade, still stands today as a private home at 131 Navesink Avenue.

As mentioned earlier, clubs were an integral draw bringing society visitors to Highlands. The second club in town was the Jackson Club, inspired by the prestige of the Neptune Club. Its members came in 1866, when the new steamboat and railroad afforded easy transportation from New York to Highlands. Initially, they summered in the hotels along the water, and then in 1868, the club leased property from Peter F. Schenck and erected a wooden clubhouse along the river just north of the present bridge. A few years later, the club of affluent New Yorkers purchased lots on the Shrewsbury River and built its clubhouse there. This was long before any streets were laid out in this part of town, which was prone to flooding and large standing pools of water. Eventually, Shrewsbury Avenue was constructed, and with Bay Avenue and Miller Street, it delineated the triangle of the Kay and Cornwell tract. Jackson Street, constructed later, ran from the location of the Jackson Club on Shrewsbury Avenue to Bay Avenue. Early in the next century, the Jackson Club became the Jackson Hotel, open to the general public, and was a longtime favorite of summer and day tourists until its destruction by fire around 1960.

The third private club to come to the Highlands was the exclusive Water Witch Club, so named by its 50 well-educated gentlemen charter members after Cooper's novel *The Water Witch, or the Skimmer of the Seas*, which so perfectly described, with recognizable detail, the geography of the area. The ruins of the so-called Water Witch Hotel were prominent in 1895 just across Navesink Avenue from the planned entrance to the Water Witch Park. The members adopted by-laws and elected their first officers in a meeting at the Surf House in the Highland Beach resort on Sandy Hook, across from Highlands. The club itself had purchased its vast estate and laid out building lots to be sold to members. A map filed with the Monmouth County clerk in 1895 shows the club's boundaries and plans for development. It included all the land of today's Monmouth Hills Association south of Navesink Avenue, as well as all the extensive area of lower Highlands commonly referred to as the Water Witch section. In the area of today's Huddy Park, the club planned to have its own electric power plant, water system, and sewer plant. Along the water, the club's leaders had laid out bathing lots, a private yacht pavilion, and both a private and public bathing area.

While the development of the lower area (with many street names taken from the novel, such as Barberie, Seadrift, and Water Witch) would have to wait until the next century, the hillside lots were developed despite the period's economic sluggishness and in 1899 had some 12 homes built around the Water Witch Clubhouse, all enjoying spectacular vistas as far as Long Island. Ferdinand Fish (an appropriate name!) was the club's president and motive force in the early years, marketing the club's properties from an office on Broadway in New York and from his local office, still standing since 1895 but now a charming private home located at the corner of Linden and Water Witch Avenues in Highlands. Water Witch Club (later Monmouth Hills) always maintained an association with Highlands but was not included in the borough created in 1900. Lower Water Witch had to wait until 1914 to join the Borough of Highlands. Even today, Monmouth Hills, although part of Middletown Township, is included in the 07732 Highlands postal zip code.

Two other Highlands industries existed simultaneous with the clamming and tourism, less well known but not less interesting from a local history point of view.

The one industry was a tie-in with the cities from which the tourists escaped—cord wood cutting. The stoves, furnaces, and fireplaces, even those using coal, in the cities required dry kindling wood to begin a fire. Highlands was a major supplier to the cities' markets. The cord wood was taken from the woods in the hills, where it was cut and split to a useful size and then was carried by wagon down the old "wood road" to the edge of the river. Here, it was stacked in cords, allowed to further dry, and awaited shipment to the city. Sometimes it was stored in anticipation of a better price, sometimes until shipping was convenient for the owner of one of the old-style Shrewsbury sailing sloops that continued to serve the city. The old "wood road" can still be located today in a gully running from the top of Portland Road near the entrance to Hartshorne Woods Park down to the river's beach.

The other industry was more in the way of a small factory or manufacturing plant. It was located along the Shrewsbury River just within Highlands in a place commonly called Greenland or Greenland Bank. The first time one hears of the "fertilizer factory" is with the telling of an interesting related story of Eleanor Thompson Benton, daughter of Joseph Thompson, the hotel owner in Highlands:

> An incident that brought many people to Highlands was the death of two large whales which lost their way in the Shrewsbury River in the early 1850s. They got on a sand bar opposite the Highlands, where they died. They were floated across to Highlands where they were placed in a large tent and sightseers had to pay to look at them. They were later floated to "Greenland" about a mile from Water Witch and made into fertilizer. I remember having taken a bath [bathing or swimming] in the river where the whales were exhibited.

This factory in 1860 was owned by a Highlands man named Louis Harper, who was a 56-year-old professional geologist and chemist with $25,000 in personal wealth, according to the 1860 U.S. census register. His factory plant supervisor, Hazen Pomeroy, age 26, lived with Harper and his family, as did Harper's younger brother, Adolphus. They employed local Highlands men to assist in the operation of turning schools of chemically rich mossbunker or menhaden, so abundant in the Sandy Hook and Raritan Bays at that time, into fertilizer, upon which the farms of the Bayshore and the rest of Monmouth County depended.

The fish element was combined with green marl, sometimes called green marl sand because it was excavated from extensive deposits found along the bayshore beaches from Keyport to the Highlands, with the heaviest concentrations being in Atlantic Highlands and Highlands. Highlands did not have a monopoly on the fertilizer business, for over in Atlantic Highlands, perhaps no more than a mile to the north from the Highlands plant, two similar factories operated on the beach near Sears Landing until 1880, when they were forced to close due as much to the complaints of residents about the foul odors as to the expense of shipping the fertilizers. The Highlands fertilizer factory continued to operate as late as 1888.

Remains of the North America *wrecked on shore on February 13, 1843, in Shrewsbury Inlet opposite Plum Island with 510 immigrants dead and 89 rescued by Life Saving Stations No. 1 and No. 2. This vessel and the* Kate Markee *(April 12, 1894) were two of the the 875 ships wrecked along Sandy Hook between 1640 and 1935.*

Highlands, close by the sea, yet protected from its full-powered wrath by Sandy Hook, has been witness to many shipwrecks along the peninsula. Between the time of the settlement of the Highlands in 1678 and 1935, a total of 875 ships had been wrecked from Sandy Hook to Cape May, with 84 wrecks and 544 lives lost just on Sandy Hook alone. The relatively low death rate was due to the almost superhuman efforts of the local men at Life Saving Stations No. 1 and No. 2 on Sandy Hook and also to the fact that most of the wrecks were of commercial vessels with small well-trained crews. The two exceptions were the *North America* (510 passengers lost on Sandy Hook off Plum Island) and the *New Era* (north Long Branch).

One story, in particular, highlights the dangers of the sea and the outright bravery of Highlands men. The four-masted schooner *Kate Markee*, loaded with paving stones and out of Fall River, Massachusetts, bound for Philadelphia, was thoroughly destroyed and all aboard, Captain Daniel Handy and seven crewmen, were drowned at Highland Beach in a savage gale April 11, 1894. When the storm raged at the height of its fury with hurricane-force rain, snow, and wind, driving huge waves that beat with terrifying strength on the beach, Jersey Central Railroad agent A.H. Bernadon spotted the ship in distress and telegraphed the Western Union Marine observer on Sandy Hook, who notified Highlands Captain Trevonian H. Patterson at Life Saving Station No. 1; he, in turn, telephoned Captain J.W. Edwards at station No. 2 at Spermaceti Cove.

When the two Life Saving Crews of eight men each arrived at Highland Beach with all their equipment, except their boats, which were useless in raging surf, the *Kate Markee* was in peril. Her crew were in the rigging in order to escape the fury of the waves, hoping and praying help would arrive in time. The men of Station No. 3 in Sea Bright came alone, having had to abandon their equipment to be able to make the journey at all. Three lines were fired by the surfmen; one parted; one caught between two of the four masts out of reach of two men in the mizzen rigging; one caught between another two masts again out of reach of three men in the foretop mast. Three men were clinging to the bowsprit. The bow suddenly lurched under the water as a huge wave raised the stern, snapping the bowsprit and washing the hapless three men into the savage boiling foam. The ship rolled over from side to side and the port mast stays snapped sending the five men up in the rigging into the water, never to be seen again, alive or dead.

Of the three men from the bowsprit, two reappeared; one was spotted struggling to grasp part of a splintered mast and losing his grip he vanished from sight; the other, a large and powerful man, had jumped from the bowsprit as it snapped. The man struggled with all his might to get to shore, and even was in waist-deep water a short distance from the Life Saving crews, but they did not have another charge to shoot a rope to him and could not throw a rope by hand into the overwhelming fierce force of the wind. They watched the man, helpless, for a few seconds, as Charles Pederson, another Highlands man tied a line about himself and started into the raging surf toward the victim. But then, the fated sailor disappeared, sucked out by the undertow, the last of eight. The 142-foot vessel broke up—rather, was ground up in the jaws of the storm—and by 10 o'clock, the *Kate Markee* was no more.

The bold Charles Pederson, a 40-year-old, 1868 immigrant boatman from Sweden, after the storm subsided, returned to Caroline, his wife of two years, at their home in Highlands near the railroad station where the heroic rescue attempt had first begun.

Some 60 years later, Highlands resident and author Fletcher Pratt mentioned the incident in the town's golden anniversary publication of 1950 and called attention to the many unique paving stones gathered over the years from the beach and placed about town, the only things surviving from the fated *Kate Markee*, otherwise long forgotten.

In 1875, the New York and Sandy Hook telegraph company was absorbed by the Western Union Telegraph Company, which had a wooden structure housing an observation tower and agents' quarters (constructed August 15, 1875, at a cost of $2,950) on a bluff just below the government property at the Twin Lights. It was located below and a bit south of the south tower so that it would not interfere with the lighthouse beacons. Clearly money was to be made in the reporting of ship arrivals, and in 1895, a rival set up its own tower just below the north tower of Twin Lights. The first operator of this Postal Telegraph Marine Observation station was Stephen Murray. He got along well with his competitor, Edward McCann, and even communicated with him on the telegraph via New York! He serviced different ships from those of his rival company, yet at times covered for him. Murray was deserving of two important achievements: first, it was he who telegraphed Marconi's radio reports on the America's Cup Race of 1899 to New York; and second, it was he who became the father of the first twins (girls born in May 1900) in the new Borough of Highlands after March 22, 1900. His rival at Western Union, Edward McCann, and his wife, Annie, were the parents of the first child, Frances (born April 1900), born in the new borough.

Murray used to live down on 159 Navesink Avenue, renting the house that is today's OLPH convent. However, after the Marconi Radio company moved its ship-to-shore radio-telegraph operation to near Belmar in 1907, the Postal Telegraph Company purchased the Marconi house and moved it adjacent to its steel observation tower to be Murray's home.

In 1933, Western Union, which bought out the competing Postal Telegraph Company operations nation-wide, closed the marine observation facilities on Twin Lights. The old Western Union structure was razed, the Postal Telegraph steel tower was dismantled, and the old Marconi house (still standing today, but in deplorable condition) was sold to Manny and Pearl (Murray) Masciale to become their home.

Considered the "father of radio," Guglielmo Marconi was just 25 years old when he left his native Italy, where he had studied physics at the University of Bologna. He had refined the early electro-magnetic work done by Heinrich Hertz and devised a practical radio antenna. In 1895, he had sent wireless signals covering more than a mile, and in early 1899, he had utterly astounded the world by sending wireless radio signals across the English channel. His wireless communication system was rejected by the Italian government, but in 1896, he secured a British patent and financial backing for his Marconi Wireless Telegraphy Company.

Marconi came to New York at the invitation of James Gordon Bennett, owner of the *New York Herald* newspaper, in order to use his wireless apparatus to report on the upcoming America's Cup yacht races off Sandy Hook. Marconi's assistant, William Bradfield, set off straight-away by steamboat to the Highlands. Marconi chose to work on the Twin Lights hill, the highest point directly along the Atlantic coast and the first sight of America the young Italian experimenter had when arriving from Europe. Bradfield set up the antenna mast with its array of wires and the radio receiver atop the hill just adjacent to the north tower. One transmitter was aboard the steamboat *Ponce* with another on the steamer *Grande Duchesse* chartered to follow the races.

Marconi poses with radio equipment he developed and used at Highlands for commercial wireless communication between 1899 and 1907.

All six of the America's Cup Races from 1893 through 1920 were held in the ocean waters off Sandy Hook easily within sight from most places in the Highlands. While the very best spot to watch the action of the yachts competing for the prized cup and the national prestige was aboard one of the hundreds of spectator boats almost on the course itself, the next best vantage point was atop one of the hills in Highlands, the higher above sea level the better, of course. Mt. Mitchill or the land around the Twin Lights gave ideal vistas and were free of charge.

The races drew very large crowds to Highlands near the end of summer. They were the most exciting sporting events ever witnessed in American waters. The hotels extended their seasons and boarding houses and bungalows practically bulged, overwhelmed with hordes of visitors who, at times, would be forced to sleep on porches and even on the beach itself. Extra steamboats were put in service and special and extra trains came from the city directly or met the boat trains at Atlantic Highlands, depositing race spectators and bettors, gentlemen and ladies as well, by the thousands to spend the day in Highlands just to watch the big races, have a picnic, relax, and enjoy the day.

Before the races, however, Commodore George Dewey triumphantly returned to New York on September 30, 1899, in parade review after his Spanish-American War victories in Manila Bay in the Philippines. In Highlands, Marconi received reports on the progress of the warship and steamer parade. These reports were relayed to the land-line telegrapher, Stephen Murray, the Postal Telegraph agent, who sent them in a blur of Morse code dots and dashes to the anxious editors waiting at the *Herald* offices. They witnessed communications history being made as Marconi literally changed the world that day!

The artist of this Harper's Weekly *of July 29, 1889, used his imagination to create this aerial view of the the America's Cup race course off Sandy Hook for that year.*

Next, all attention was focused and bets were laid down on the America's Cup Races to run October 16 and 17, after a two-week delay due to bad weather. The prestige of the United States of America was at stake at the racecourse finish line. It was the America's *Columbia*, owned by J.P. Morgan, against Thomas Lipton's *Shamrock* from Britain's Northern Ireland. The excitement was intense!

Marconi had his equipment there atop the hill near the Twin Lights north tower. Bradfield began receiving Morse code reports from Marconi aboard the *Grande Duchesse* in the thick of the competition at sea. Reports on the status of the *Columbia* and *Shamrock* rapidly flew through the air and electrified the small crowd of bystanders hearing the bzt-bzt-bzt-bzzzt of the wireless spark gap transmitter. Instantly, this was received in Highlands and wire telegraphed to the writers at the *New York Herald*. All the other newspapers were scooped, thanks to Marconi's ingenious wireless radio system.

Marconi continued his experiments with ever-improving equipment. Nonetheless, he had a difficult time convincing American financial investors, since other scientists maintained Marconi's wireless was limited to relatively short and line-of-sight distances. Universal adoption of his devices came soon, for in December 1901, Marconi spanned the Atlantic Ocean, from Cornwall, England, to St. John's, Newfoundland, with Morse code signals sent with his wireless radio system. His Marconi Company equipment and operators increasingly were placed aboard ocean-going steamships, and in 1909, saved two shiploads of passengers from death in a collision at sea.

That same year, Marconi received the scientific world's greatest tribute, the Nobel Prize in Physics, for his work in wireless communication. He died on July 20, 1937, in Rome. The next day, all radio stations world-wide went silent for two minutes in tribute to the man who, from a hilltop in Highlands, brought victory for the yacht *Columbia*, victory for the *Herald*, and victory for Marconi and his wireless radio communication.

The first seven America's Cup yacht races, starting in 1870, were run in New York's Lower Bay and always generated exceptional interest amongst the city's socially elite sportsman, as well as the everyday working and betting man. The following of the race in 1876, when America was celebrating its centennial of independence, was especially avid, especially in the large Irish immigrant neighborhoods, although the New York Yacht Club's *Madeleine* was defending, not against the traditional English challenger, but against British Canada's *Countess of Dufferin*.

An especially exciting race from the view point of the Irish Americans, or rather, a series of races, for the cup was the challenge of Sir Thomas Lipton's *Shamrock I*, representing Northern Ireland in 1899, the year Marconi's new wireless telegraph reported the minute by minute results. Lipton lost then, and again in 1901, 1903, 1920, and 1930, but good-naturedly, it was always said.

Highlands native Edna McGuire Kruse used to talk of Lipton stopping his boat at the Highlands and coming into the old McGuire house—opposite Bahrs Landing restaurant—or later on to the Kruse Pavilion for a quick glass of refreshment (not a tea!). She remembered him as a "tall man, with a tanned face, steel gray hair, and a pleasure to talk to, a laugh-easy gentleman with a sly smile, honestly kind."

Around the turn of the century, the Highlands hills were populated by a whole constellation of theater stars, famous New York City actors and actresses, who found there

The famous comic actor Neil Burgess is depicted here on a calling card showing him as a stage artist literally creating the role "Vim," which made him rich and famous.

an ideal summer resort. Here, they built regal summer get-away "cottages," where they enjoyed cool and refreshing breezes, grand vistas of the ocean, the bays, and rivers, and awesome views of Far Rockaway, Coney Island, and the city of Manhattan, to which they were connected by steamboat or train in a little more than an hour's time.

In this summer actors colony, located below the Twin Lights in Highlands, were such notables as Thomas Wallace Keene, who starred in tragic roles including *Othello*, *Richard III*, and *Hamlet* with high acclaim for his "majestic method" and his handsome appearance, and John and Nellie McHenry Webster, who enjoyed success in both comedy and drama on extensive road tours of the United States, Canada, Europe, and Australia. Others in the theatrical landscape were John and Cornelia Wheelock, Horace McVicker, W.A. Hayden, and J.S. Hoffman (later a borough councilman), all famous on the New York stage. Of all of these, the one in the brightest limelight was Neil Burgess.

Burgess's stage career began humbly at age 19 in varied vaudeville acts in the Boston area. Good fortune, appropriately, came one night in Providence. He was the stage manager with a touring company playing *The Quiet Family* and the actress in the lead role of Mrs. Barnaby Bibbs was taken ill and Burgess was forced to improvise the part. With that one night, his stage career was exclusively devoted to caricatures and burlesques of eccentric and garrulous elderly women, "old widdy women," they were called. The audiences roared and the critics generally approved every comic extravagance of feminine voice, gesture, and costume Burgess invented for his 1879 roles in *Vim, or, a Visit to Puffy Farm* and *Widow Bedott, or, a Hunt for a Husband*.

His most popular part was playing Auntie Abigail Prue in *The County Fair*, which was a play written specifically for him (1888) by Charles Barnard of Burlington, New Jersey. The play opened on March 5, 1889, in New York at Proctor's Fifth Avenue Theatre and went through more than 5,000 performances. The popularity of this play was due in part, at least, to the stunning effect of Barnard (as inventor) and Burgess's (as financial backer) turntable device, which allowed horses to gallop full speed on the stage as part of the action. This same device was used, with great profit for Burgess and Barnard, in the spectacular chariot race scenes in productions of *Ben Hur*. His success brought him popular adulation, critical respect, and unprecedented wealth as the highest-paid actor, comic or tragic, of the time—all for cross-dressing and female impersonation, his singular specialty.

Burgess purchased a place in the Highlands hills, where in 1883, along Navesink Avenue, contractor J.D. Brown built his palatial mansion—turreted towers and all—called *Tempus Fugit* (Latin for "time flies"), according to plans, drawings, and specifications prepared by Charles and George Palliser, architects renowned for their late Victorian designs and creations. The house stood to the west of the grand old hotels, the Victoria, the Monmouth, and the Highland House, near the bridge until *Tempus Fugit* disappeared in a spectacular blaze of fire and sparks in the late 1960s.

In a similar manner, Burgess's fortunes went up in the smoke of injudicious and unprofitable theatrical investments and ill-advised real estate speculations in the Highlands hills. For example, after considerable financial outlay, he eventually received a patent in 1905 for an "apparatus which can simulate the effect and sound of large crowds, as at the race track in the grandstands." Burgess hoped to cash in on an expected real estate boom in the hills about Highlands and consequently purchased two large tracts of land that totaled more than a dozen acres and stretched from Navesink Avenue, or Route 36, down to the Shrewsbury River's edge, located at Rogers and North Linden Avenues. The price was $7,500, a princely sum in 1891 dollars.

The Neil Burgess cottage was designed by architects Charles and George Palliser and constructed in 1883 on Navesink Avenue next to the Highland House.

Burgess attempted a tour of England with his *County Fair* in 1897, and it was panned at most every presentation, as the British theater public failed to understand and appreciate his special form of American humor. With diminished financial resources, he was forced to rely more and more upon the generosity of his mother-in-law, Ann Stoddard, who came from a distinguished family of actors and possessed impressive financial acumen.

Tragedy sucked the comedy out of Neil Burgess, when his wife, Mary, died in 1905. Demoralized and suffering from ill health, yet not ready to surrender, Burgess took a condensed version of *The County Fair* onto the vaudeville stage. His last years were a professional and financial struggle. Finally, in 1910, he was laid to rest atop the hill at All Saints Episcopal Church, beneath a magnificent granite and bronze monument displaying the portrait bust of Neil Burgess gazing out upon the hills of Highlands.

William Sandlass's Highland Beach excursion resort was decidedly one of the several elements that influenced the successful development of Highlands as a major tourist destination. This was so, although it must be remembered that it was not strictly speaking ever a part of Highlands, lying as it did on Sandy Hook across the Shrewsbury from town. It covered an area from ocean to river, in today's terms, stretching from Something Fishy north to within about 25 feet of the wall of the red-brick building, the old WW II Provost Marshall's office and Gateway's Fee office today. It received its name in 1879 from the New Jersey Southern Railroad's Highland Beach station, the first stop on the railroad link between the New York steamboat dock at Horse Shoe Cove and Long Branch. More incredible still, the whole resort complex was in Ocean Township, that is, until the Borough of Seabright (Sea Bright is an alternative spelling) annexed it on March 31, 1909.

The gravity railroad was one of the thrilling attractions offered at the extremely popular Highland Beach Resort of William Sandlass. A car of the government steam railroad line going from Highland Station to Fort Hancock and the Proving Grounds is visible at right.

Soon its owner, William Sandlass, bringing with him over a quarter of a million dollars in ratables, won election as mayor of the borough.

Since the railroad running to Long Branch only was interested in a right-of-way, it sold in 1880 all the strip of land extending south of the government lands of Sandy Hook for about 1.3 miles. Mr. and Mrs. Reckless of Red Bank bought and in turn sold it in May 1881 to a development company, the Highland Beach Association, or the Highlands Beach Improvement Company, headed by real estate magnate Ferdinand Fish (of Water Witch Club). His promotional brochures and posters in the city in an attempt to sell building lots touted the place as the nearest ocean beach in Jersey from New York and opposite the Highlands of Navesink thoroughly familiar to and heavily frequented by the city crowds.

The sales did not meet Fish's expectations, forcing him to sell even his own summer mansion called the Aquarium and the company to sell in December 1887 to William Sandlass the northern half of all the lots. Inspired by the resort at Manhattan Beach on Coney Island, Sandlass constructed his Highland Beach.

The resort offered both surf and still bathing (*i.e.* ocean and river swimming). Bathing costumes were available for ladies and gentlemen to rent for a small charge. The bathing fee was 25¢ and family dressing rooms were 50¢ per day. One could use hammocks, play lawn-tennis, quoits, and croquet, or shoot rifles and bows-and-arrows, or ride the carousel for a small fee. Bowling, dancing, and concerts of popular music (sacred music on Sundays, of course) were available each day throughout the summer season. There were sailboats and canoes to rent, as well as carriages to hire for an afternoon drive into the Highlands, Atlantic Highlands, Rumson, and even Long Branch. The resort's dining room and bars were great attractions—Bass Ale, Guinness' Brown Stout, or Ballantine Pale Extra only 15¢ a bottle and a hearty "Shrewsbury Dinner" featuring clam chowder, steamer clams, fish boiled, baked, or fried, roast meat, corn, lobster or crab salad, clam fritters, fruit or pastry, bread and butter, and coffee for only $1. Later, in the next century, the Bamboo Room and Garden featured an exotic ambiance for drinks and dinner, and even an airdrome for the outdoor showing of moving pictures in the 1920s.

The place was extremely popular, even before its development as a resort under Sandlass, from the 1850s as evidenced from an 1857 *Balou's* illustrated article on blue fishing from the surf, which showed large crowds of ladies and men picnicking, fishing, and generally enjoying the natural beach. New Yorkers deluged the resort, arriving by the steamboat-rail connection at Highland Station, coming by the steamboats docking at Highlands and a stroll across the bridge, and after 1892, when the steamboat-rail connection shifted from Sandy Hook to Atlantic Highlands, by the steamboats *Sea Bird* and *Albertina*, first docking at the Highlands Beach pier and then crossing the river to the Highlands docks. Crowds seeking the pleasure of a beach and resort also poured out of the interior of Monmouth County, coming via Red Bank and intermediate stops on the several small steam launches loaded with up to 125 day tourists each boat run. The *Jersey Lily*, *Our Mary*, *Leon Abbett*, *Highland Beach*, *Shrewsbury*, and *Navesink* were the names of boats in this lucrative service. The year all six operated, they made seven trips (at 25¢ round trip) to the resort each day in the summer, bringing as many as 3,000 persons a day!

The place was a gold mine for Sandlass and for the Highlands hotels (Sandlass even attempted to purchase Thompson's Pavilion, the East View House, and Swift's Pavilion in

These well-dressed New York ladies and their children await one of the steamboats running from Manhattan to the dock at Horseshoe Cove.

1888), boarding houses, and businesses across the river, which accommodated the overflow crowds and provided alternative activities, both in the late nineteenth century and in the twentieth century up until after the Jersey Central's abandonment of the bridge and line to Long Branch in 1947. At this time, the Highland Beach resort, drastically reduced in reputation and numbers of buildings, essentially became the Sandlass Beach Club, which operated as a private beach club until its last season in 1961. The bathhouses and changing booths were razed by Sandy Hook State Park workers in 1962. Today, even the old Bamboo Room (once a state park maintenance building) is gone, and only the old William Sandlass house, a residence of Gateway workers, remains to remind today's generations of all the facilities and amusements that once stood there.

With the fort at Sandy Hook left essentially incomplete and ungarrisoned after the Civil War, the people at Highlands must have appreciated the lull in activity after the end of each season, much as many of today's residents still can remember how peaceful the little town would become after the summer was over; after all, the city people went back home. However, much of that off-season tranquillity disappeared with the arrival of first, the weapons testing program, and second, the rapid activation of an even larger fort at Sandy Hook.

The Sandy Hook Proving Grounds were officially established by the secretary of war on August 7, 1874, and within two years after that, the people living in Highlands knew their off-seasonal peace was gone. The rapid advance in heavy weapons technology of the Civil War years, which doomed traditional fortifications like the one never completed on Sandy Hook, accelerated even faster and required a place suited for the testing of new weapons before government acceptance and purchase. Sandy Hook was a logical choice, being already almost totally government owned, being well situated near New York and Washington, D.C., having a sound railroad system well established as far as the Horse Shoe Cove to provide movement of heavy weapons and munitions as well as civilian day laborers, and being reasonably undeveloped. Its one drawback was the extensive shipping activity on all sides of the peninsula. With all precautions taken, loss of life and property was minimal.

Highlands, the closest town, all in all, despite the fireworks and roaring blasts from guns and rockets, benefited from the employment provided in government work and from the revenue brought to its businesses by the civilians and soldiers working and stationed there. Fort Hancock was born October 30, 1895, with the army's general order number 57, naming the Sandy Hook installation after Major General Winfield Scott Hancock (1824-1886), the capable leader of Union infantry forces at Fredericksburg, Chancellorsville, and Gettysburg and Presidential candidate in 1882 against Garfield. The Highlands Civil War veterans of the 29th Regiment, who served in the first two battles and were members of the Clinton B. Fisk Post of the Grand Army of the Republic since 1892, must have cheered their approval of the post's creation and naming. However, in the long relationship between Highlands and Fort Hancock from 1895 until its final closing in 1974, at times the people of town were not cheerful.

Major General Winfield Scott Hancock was a West Point graduate who commanded an infantry division with distinction during the Battles of Fredericksburg and Chancellorsville in the Civil War. At Gettysburg, his repulse of Pickett's charge assured the Union victory.

At any rate, the development of Fort Hancock brought Highlands benefits of employment during and after construction and business in town many times what came from the Proving Grounds. In its first five years, there was constructed in brick a Herculean number of buildings, including 18 married officer houses, a dozen married sergeant houses, bachelor officers' quarters, 4 huge enlisted men's barracks, non-commissioned officers' quarters, stables, a large hospital, a guard house, and the post headquarters. During the same period, the granite blocks, bricks, and concrete of the old Civil War–era fort had to be removed, and massive amounts of concrete were poured to fashion 12 coastal defense gun batteries for the protection of New York and its harbor.

Although Fort Hancock brought many benefits, Highlands, like so many small towns, suffered in the late nineteenth century from a lack of some larger city civic conveniences. Thomas H. Leonard, founder and first mayor of Atlantic Highlands, wrote a brief summary of Parkertown village in neighboring Highlands or Seaside, alluding to the relationship of Highlands to the township government in Middletown in 1895:

> From this humble beginning has sprung up a thrifty village, with two churches
> and a number of stores, and resident accommodations, with a population that
> commands the respect of, at least, the politicians around election time.

He suggested Highlands was avoided by people in nearby towns and neglected by government authorities responsible for collecting taxes and maintaining the town's streets and roads.

According to a *Register* article of July 4, 1888, Miller Street—one of three roads leading to lower Highlands—had become the *bête noire* of Middletown township, continually washing out in heavy rainstorms and becoming unusable even for school kids attempting

Streets had dirt surfaces at this time and were periodically oiled or sprinkled with water to reduce the dust. This view, looking south, shows Miller Street.

This engraving from Harper's New Monthly Magazine *in September 1879 dramatically captures the Twin Lights and many summer residents enjoying Highlands.*

to climb the hillside to get to the grammar school on Navesink Avenue at Miller Street. Unsatisfactory quick-fix repairs only produced a constant barrage of complaints from concerned Highlands leaders to the governing committee. Finally, after many meetings discussing Miller Street, the committee agreed to properly rebuild the road.

From the time the Central Railroad of New Jersey first came through Highlands in 1892, leaders in the community complained to the railroad company and to the township committee about the many pools of standing water—an unhealthy situation—along the railroad right-of-way, asking that they be drained and filled in, all without satisfactory result. They complained to the Monmouth County freeholders directly, through the township committee officials, and through state representatives from Atlantic Highlands, about the poor conditions of the county roads—Linden Avenue, Bay Avenue, Navesink Avenue—and about the deteriorated condition of the county-owned bridge across the Shrewsbury River, both before and after the Central Railroad rebuilt the pedestrian and vehicle crossing in 1892.

There was much dissatisfaction, soon to be resolved in an extraordinary way at the beginning of the next century.

6. THE BOROUGH'S FIRST 40 YEARS

For the people of the Borough of Highlands, the twentieth century has meant 100 years of independence—a century of overall progress, interrupted at times by periods of retrogression and deterioration of past achievements. They lived through the creation of a new political entity, the borough, and worked hard with their dedicated public officials for one selfless goal, the genuine improvement of Highlands, always mindful of the initial and constant critics of the place and its people and the need to silence them by proving them wrong. It was a struggle crowned with general success by the time one third of the new century had passed. The town boasted paved streets with sidewalks, water, sewer, gas and lighting systems, police, fire, first aid, and municipal services, ample employment opportunities, even during the Depression, and a solid business district, all fed and financed by a summer resort and tourist trade from the cities. Could places like Belford, Leonardo, or New Monmouth in Middletown Township boast of comparable progress?

During a New Year's Eve celebration in Highlands on December 31, 1899, many of the leading men had been talking about how something must be done, and done soon, to correct the inequities the town's residents and businessmen suffered at the hands of the politicians in Middletown. They made toasts to better times, to better conditions for the village of Seaside. All the men there must have made New Year's resolutions to build a town they could be proud to call their own. It was a new year and a new century dawning, the twentieth century, filled with optimism and great expectations all across America. They saw no reason why they would not succeed in starting a borough. After all, Atlantic Highlands, their neighbor, had done just this in 1887.

Charles T. Maison and David M. Miller were the leaders of the group planning for independence from Middletown. The others were Frederick E. Johnson, John L. Johnson, James Taylor, John W. Taylor, Joseph Brown, Ivy Brown, John H. Foster, John W. Foster, Samuel L. Wilson, Lewis Parker, Mahlon Burdge, Samuel C. Burdge, Thomas Hennessey, and Bendet Rosenblum. They held a meeting over in Atlantic Highlands with State Assemblyman Charles R. Snyder. They reviewed the years of dissatisfaction the people of Seaside and Highlands felt, how they saw themselves orphaned governmentally and financially abused at tax time, and how far removed they were physically and politically from the government decision-making over in Middletown's Town Hall. Miller, a lifelong clammer who supported his wife and six children on the river, pointed out that $1,900 used to be sent to Middletown in taxes and only $500 came back in services. This was

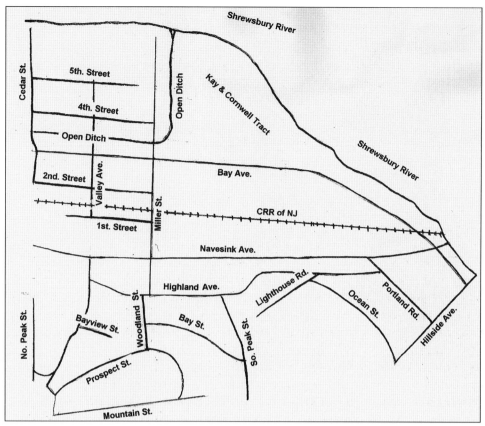

This map shows the Borough of Highlands at the time of its incorporation on March 22, 1900, when the small town had a population of 1,228.

enough justification for secession and independence from Middletown Township to suit any reasonable, hard-working man of the times. Mr. Snyder agreed and drew up the petition for secession, which all 16 men signed boldly, as men in 1776 did on the Declaration of Independence, taking the first steps toward independence. Snyder drew up and introduced the bill of incorporation of the Borough of Highlands (Assembly Bill No. 181 of 1900), with the co-sponsorship of Senator C. Asa Francis, to the New Jersey State Legislature on February 13, 1900.

On March 22, 1900, Seaside and Highlands became a borough independent from Middletown Township, for it was on this day in the state capitol at Trenton that the bill of incorporation of the Borough of Highlands was passed by the legislature and signed into law by Governor Foster Voorhees.

The *New York Times* was selling for 1¢ in the city and 2¢ there in New Jersey's newest municipality. On its front page, the headlines recorded stories regarding the British and Boer conflict in South Africa, Admiral George Dewey's triumphal return from his victories in the Spanish-American War, and the planned new canal in Central America. These were some of the great events of the nation and the world reported that day. Hundreds of events of lesser significance took place that day amongst the people of

David M. Miller, leader of the movement for independence from Middletown, was the first mayor and served from April 24, 1900, to March 15, 1902.

Highlands, but these were never recorded. There was no fanfare, no parade, no speeches in Highlands that day. Life went on as it had always gone for Maggie Hayes, Barney Creighton, Mary Parker, Stephen Scalia, Bendet Rosenblum, William Washington, Sarah Cottrell, and George Hartsgrove—except that day, Highlands was in charge of its own destiny.

The *Monmouth Press*, on March 31, 1900, carried the following story entitled "Highlands Borough?":

> The people of Seaside have succeeded in securing incorporation and their new borough will be known by the name of Highlands. The movement to incorporate has seemed to many outside of the new borough lines to be one of the wildest municipal projects conceivable. The present voters of the locality do not rank high as taxpayers or moralists. They have scarcely ordinary educational qualifications. They have few of the safeguards to prevent it becoming a hotbed of corruption and an opportunity for all sorts of schemes and shysters. Does this not look like folly of the maddest sort?
>
> But now the act is the LAW and the situation has changed. The new borough will have the chance to prove the critics wrong. Highlands, with self-government, can, of course, surprise the world, despite critics who may take it for granted that the new borough will be a sorry failure.
>
> But the enthusiasm which secured establishment of the new municipality will be constantly required to make the borough government a success. There is a

lawlessness associated with the locality. Sunday liquor selling and drunkenness are perennial complaints. Squabbles and bastardy proceedings have prejudiced the outside world against Highlands for generations.

Yet there are those who maintain that Highlands will effect important reforms. It is hopeful that they are right for Highlands certainly has the opportunity to vindicate itself. Far be it from this newspaper to hinder advancement and discourage honest effort for improvement. Our hearty co-operation is assured to every worker for a better Highlands. Aid and encouragement for the worthy ends achievable are the proper watchwords now!

Detractors and complainers exist in all human affairs. Yet these critics are always on the periphery, never in the center of affairs where action for progress initiates, never in the center where the following first leaders of the Borough of Highlands stood firm after the first election. In this first election, 186 votes were cast out of 248 registered voters on April 24, 1900. The following are the results of that historic election: mayor, David M. Miller; councilmen, John T. Johnson, Mahlon Burdge, Lewis F. Parker, John N. Riker, and Richard Mount; tax assessor, Abram J. Parker; tax collector, Charles T. Maison; justice of the peace, John H. Foster; commissioners of appeals, Bernard Creighton, Stephen Foster, and Reuben Parker; appointed borough clerk, Jesse L. Sculthorpe; appointed chief of police, Thomas Derby; appointed marshal, Job G. Liming; appointed borough physician, Dr. R.C. Andrews; and borough attorney, Charles R. Snyder. The council approved as official newspapers the *Journal* of Atlantic Highlands and the *Monmouth Press* of Red Bank and established the following committees: streets, lighting, finance, licenses, auditing, police and jail, printing, and supplies.

The new officials of the Borough of Highlands quickly did some figuring of the comparative benefits of a borough government from a financial point of view. They calculated they would raise from taxes in 1900 the sum of $800, keeping the tax rate the same as the old Middletown tax rate. The borough would get from licenses about $1,100, thus making a total of $1,900 the new borough had to spend. They were very excited and encouraged because this was almost four times the amount ever spent under township control in Highlands and because the taxes would not increase.

The new borough was a tiny town of just 1,228 persons, according to the U.S. census taken June 4, 1900. The boundaries in 1900 were approximately as follows: the Shrewsbury River, Hillside Avenue and continuing on this line up to the government property at Twin Lights, Mountain Street, North Peak Street and continuing on this line across Navesink Avenue down to approximately Cedar Street to the river.

The newly elected officials were much more concerned about the welfare and success of their borough than they were about political affiliations, loyalty, and party allegiances. The first mayor, David Miller, all the councilmen, and all the others elected to office were neither Democratic nor Republican—they were simply Highlanders! The first three administrations under Mayors David M. Miller, Charles T. Maison, and Peter M. Cornwell were apparently apolitical. It was not until 1906, under acting Mayor Harry A. Brown, that one can associate a mayor with a political party, Republican in Brown's case. After his tenure, Mayor Allan R. Reid, a declared Republican, was supported in his campaigns for two terms as mayor by both the Republicans and the Democrats, so highly was he regarded for his political honesty and integrity by voters of both political persuasions. From this point onward to modern times, Highlands politics has often been characterized by political rivalry, antagonism, and an alternation of retributive domination by one party after the other, sometimes clearly to the detriment of the town and its people.

A century ago, the town was small. Its "footprint" was less than half the size it is today. Highlands annexed neighboring lands along Portland Road and all of the Water Witch section in 1914. It was even smaller from a practical standpoint, since all the area in the triangle formed by Shrewsbury Avenue, Bay Avenue, and Miller Street (the Kay and Cornwell tract) was essentially an undeveloped swamp, which would remain that way for almost another decade. Highlands in 1900 was approximately one third its geographic size today. Further, with a 1900 population of 1,228 compared with today's roughly 5,200, Highlands of 1900 had a quarter the number of residents it has today. However, when the trains and steamboats full of city excursionists arrived each day during the summer season, the population of 1900 Highlands might swell to as many as 15,000. Those who were not day-staying visitors would stay perhaps a week or more in one of the 13 hotels or guesthouses in town that year.

Of the total 1900 population, 98.2% were white; the small "Negro" population were all live-in servants in the several hotels along the river. The ratio of the sexes was about even,

The Sea Bird *of the Merchant Steamboat Co. carried a large number of tourists from New York to Highlands. From 1819 to 1932, Highlands was connected to the cities and their tourists via the boats until the advent of trains, trucks, buses, and automobiles.*

with 50.7% male and 49.3% female. There were 200 families or households in town, most with two parents and children, but 13% had a single parent. Of these, the number of divorcees was low (just four) and only five were separated and living apart from a spouse. Most single-parent situations were due to a death, with six times the number of widows as widowers. Most people, 36.6%, were married; of those not married, 6.9% were divorced or widowed. Children under age 18 accounted for 40.4%, with equal numbers of boys and girls. Single adults were 23% of the total population.

Of the 494 children, 40.8% were pre-school age, and school-age kids made up 41.7% between the ages of 5 and 13. High school–age children were 17.5%. Not all school-aged children actually attended either "grammar" (elementary) or high school. Only 84.8% were enrolled in classes, and 15.2% were not in school, and the majority of these were working full time as boatmen, clerks, clammers, plumbers, express drivers, teamsters (drivers of a team of horses pulling a wagon), laborers, houseworkers, waitresses, and milliners. The median age for children was 7 for boys and 7.5 for girls, while for men it was 31 and for women, 21. Only 6.9% of the adult population was at retirement age (65), and of this group, only two persons were actually retired. Of the dozen men of age 70 or higher, all were working in physically demanding jobs, such as laborer, teamster, or clammer. The oldest Highlander was a woman of 81 years, named, ironically, Ann Young, who had been born in Scotland in January 1819. John Druman, born in Ireland in February 1820, was the oldest man and was still working as a laborer at age 80. There were no retirement pension plans, no Social Security plans, no workmen's compensation, no health insurance, no welfare programs. There were only the worker and his family to care for each other as best they could. When they could not, there was the borough commissioner of the poor, who would periodically ask the council to approve a small amount of money to prevent starvation or freezing of a helpless person, provided he or she was not an alcoholic.

Of all the people in town, most had been born in New Jersey (74.2%), 12.8% were born in New York, and 8.2% were foreign born, with the greatest number being born in Ireland. Of the 1,228 total population in 1900, 36.2% were employed in a variety of jobs outside the home. The wives of male heads-of-household were not considered gainfully employed; they simply kept house. The Highlanders of 1900 were fully employed in work characteristic of a famous seashore and resort community. Water-related work accounted for 39.4% of all jobs and clammers made up 34%. In other work related to the river and bay, there were jobs like boatman, fisherman, bridge tender, and flagman. In accommodations-related work, 13% of all jobs were occupations such as hotel proprietor, boarding house owner, hotel manager, bartender, cook, waiter and waitress, chambermaid, laundress, and porter.

The census of 1900 reveals the kinds of shops existing in town: two butcher shops, a fruit and vegetable shop, a barber, a candy store, a millinery shop, and a shirt-manufacturing shop. In the trades, there were 12 carpenters, 2 masons, 7 plumbers, 6 painters, 6 gardeners, 9 teamsters, 2 telegraphers, a lighthouse keeper and 2 assistants, a machinist, a boat carpenter, and a printer. Also, the Central Railroad of New Jersey had eight men at the "Highland station," four engineers, a station agent, a baggage master, and two express agents.

Several indicators can be used to gauge the success of a community, such as employment rate, annual family income, level of education, ratio of home ownership (53%) to rental (47%), and literacy rate. Highlands in 1900 fares well in all but the last of these, literacy rate, or how many persons above age nine in a community can both read and write with comprehension his/her native language. At this time, almost 8% of the population were illiterate, including persons who claimed to be able to read but not write. The median age of the illiterate group was 39 years, and most of them were fully employed as laborers, clammers, or housewives.

The first ordinances enacted are often cited as instructive anecdotes from the first few years, such as Ordinance III: To Prevent and Punish Immoral Conduct; Ordinance VI: Regulating Driving and Fast Riding (setting a top speed limit of 8 m.p.h. and requiring non-horse vehicles to have a bell audible from 100 feet); Ordinance XIII (stating no horse, mule, cattle, sheep, goat, or swine are allowed to run at large in the streets); and Ordinance XVI (to prevent persons from appearing in public streets in bathing suits). As amusing as they are, they are not reflective in any special way of circumstances in Highlands. The streets were not overrun with pigs and cows, and should rather be seen as standard ordinances, typical in most cities, establishing good civic order.

By way of contrast, here are a few significant early facts, enactments, and events. In 1901, the budget was $2,051.15 collected in taxes, with $593.19 delinquent in taxes (23%). Total receipts from taxes, fees from hotels, vendors, fines, and dog licenses were $4,284.56. Total expenses were $3,705.85, leaving a surplus of $578.71. Towards the end of 1905, however, finances were not so solid as borough council stated that "All bills are to be paid, if money is available," and later "No money is on hand for any purposes." The total worth of the borough in 1906 was $453,600, including $406,850 in real estate and $46,750 in personal property.

A raging fire destroyed four to five homes and rendered homeless and destitute six families on February 17, 1904. Mayor and council acted, calling a special meeting the next day to approve taking out a $200 note from the bank and giving the money to an ad hoc committee of three councilmen to help these families cope. Next on March 14 and June 27, 1904, the First Fire Protection Ordinance was passed by mayor and council, requiring a building permit for and inspections of new and old structures with chimneys, fireplaces, flues, stoves, etc. On May 23, 1904, the Borough assumed responsibility for the Star Hook and Ladder Fire Co., bringing it under council funding and direction, and on December 23, 1907, the Columbia Hose Company No. 1 (formerly the Independent Hook and Ladder Co. No. 1) followed.

The governmental year changed when at the February 27, 1905 mayor and council meeting, it was reported by the borough attorney Snyder that the New Jersey Legislatures had abolished the spring elections, requiring all elected and appointed officials, whose terms would expire in March 1906, to continue in office through December 31, 1906, until January 1, 1907. This act made the political year the same as the calendar year.

Indications of a growing summer tourist trade appeared during this period. In 1906, the Water Witch Development Co. started marketing homes and its boat basin to city families. Martin Gerbrach opened the famous Martin House near the bridge, and Barney Creighton started the Creighton Hotel and Pavilion (later Kruse's) near the steamboat

The Jersey Central Traction Company trolley deposits visitors at the Highlands Terminus.

dock at 24 Bay Avenue. At 78 Bay Avenue, Harry Sculthorpe opened the new Highlands Auditorium Theatre (commonly called the "purple building" today) for vaudeville and moving picture shows. William H. Conners built and opened his famous resort, the Cedar Grove Hotel, in the summer of 1907 in the Water Witch section.

Starting on Saturday, September 1, 1907, the Jersey Central Traction Company ran electric trolleys to Highlands and carried tens of thousands of passengers visiting the popular shore town. The route from the Highlands began at the ticket station near today's Route 36 and Portland Road. This station survives today, thanks to the Bahrs family, as a giftshop called Strokes 'n' Stitches, providing an excellent example of how buildings from the town's past heritage can be adapted to modern use.

Today, one can accurately map out the route of the Jersey Central Traction Company trolleys by following the high-power transmission lines of the old Jersey Central Power and Light Company, now called GPU. Since the old trolleys of the Jersey Central Traction Company required overhead electric lines for power, the trolley line became a power company as well, the subsidiary Middlesex and Monmouth Electric Light, Heat and Power Company (later called Jersey Central Power and Light Company). In 1907, when the trolley company received a franchise to operate in Highlands, the power company also received a franchise from Highlands Borough to supply, erect, and maintain 45 16-candle-power streetlights for $600 annually. By 1910, it was selling electrical power to private individuals. This same year, the home at 254 Navesink Avenue (now the Water Witch House Bed and Breakfast) and the shop at 165 Bay Avenue, Johnson's Drugstore (now the Sand Dollar Card and Gift Shop), were the first in Highlands to receive the new electricity.

The trolley ran along Route 36 through Butter Milk Valley and Navesink to Atlantic Highlands and continued along Leonardville Road to Campbell's Junction, where one

A modern reminder of the trolleys of old, this quaint trolley-bus ran summers in 1999 and 2000 connecting New York City ferries with Highlands and Sandy Hook beaches and historic sites.

could switch to trolleys heading to Keansburg and Keyport or Red Bank via Middletown's Tindall Road and Route 35.

Trolley fares from Highlands were 5¢ to Atlantic Highlands, 10¢ to Campbell's Junction, 15¢ to Red Bank, and 20¢ to Keyport. Service was hourly from 7 a.m. to midnight, with trolley cars running every half-hour during the commuter hours. Many additional cars were put into service, running between the Atlantic Highlands station loop and Highlands during the summer vacation season to accommodate the vast crowds spilling from the ferryboats arriving filled with visitors wanting to come spend the day at the resorts in Highlands itself and Highland Beach on Sandy Hook.

The trolley company was a sound and practical business, which immensely benefited from the summer ridership coming from the cities via the ferries and greatly benefited the businesses along the trolley's route from Red Bank to Highlands. However, from 1919, competition from the growing number of automobiles and jitney busses and a severe decline in mass tourism due to fear of the influenza epidemic hurt the business of the trolleys. The Monmouth County Electric Company trolleys stopped running from Red Bank to Rumson and Long Branch in February 1922. The Jersey Central Traction Company abandoned its Red Bank to Highlands route a year and a half later. Its route was not quickly picked up by a bus company, and people had to wait until October 15, 1925, when the Triangle Bus Company began running the route. In 1926, the very successful Boro Busses Company of Red Bank, owned and operated by Burdge and Russell, took over the debt-ridden Triangle Company with bus route No. 4 (now New Jersey Transit Route No. 24), initially covering almost the same route as the trolley.

After an absence of nearly 80 years, "trolleys" (actually busses made to resemble the old trolleys) returned in the summer of 1999 to Highlands carrying passengers coming off the New York City ferryboats (Seastreak and Prospect Fast Ferry). Providing quaint-looking local transportation to Highlands had some vocal critics in town, but generally, it was to be commended for its attempt at helping the town's tourist image, despite under-utilization of the line by the public.

The same poles that carried the electric wires were put to use for telephone wires, and by July 1907, there were three public phones at Creighton's Hotel, Johnson's Miller Street Drugstore, and Johnson's Bridge Drugstore, from which residents could summon the police and fire department. Private residences had to wait until June 1912 for service.

Ordinances XXII and XXIII of September 23, 1907, mark the beginning of the Highlands water system, using artesian wells drilled at the southeast corner of Miller Street and Shore Drive (formerly the CRRNJ), at a bonded cost of $30,000, the town's first major expense. Highlands is a town blessed with water, water from the river, bay, ocean, and also from aquifers deep below ground and springs flowing from its hills.

One spring in the Highlands hills was famous the world over, being prominently delineated on navigational charts of the New York City area as the Water Spout. This spring has flowed unceasingly from the hillside along Bayside Drive in Atlantic Highlands about a mile from the Highlands border.

It was from this source, according to Leonard's *From Indian Trail to Electric Rail*, that sailing ships from all parts of the world procured their water supply for distant sea voyages. The water came gushing out of the rocks and was carried by pipes and troughs to the beach below to fill ships' casks. Leonard writes enthusiastically of his own personal experience as follows:

> It was a sight that would fail of description to see the fleet of the New England fishermen, numbering at certain times a year as many as 300 sail, that would harbor awhile, waiting for favorable winds. They would fill their water casks at the spout. To witness their simultaneous hoisting of sail and leaving the harbor, the scene heightened by the bright morning sun, whitening this vast expanse of sail, produced a scene of remarkable beauty not easily surpassed.

Locals in the area know the Spout better as Henry Hudson's Spring, believing that the *Half Moon* took on freshwater here after many days at sea, although Juet's journal makes no mention of the spring.

Several less famous springs flow out of the Highlands hills. These springs actually are responsible for the survival of the early fishing community in lower Highlands during the century before the town's first true water system in 1907. One located on the Miller Street hill near the water pumping plant, just below Route 36, had a wooden trough into which the water constantly flowed. There were always a few cups or glasses for any thirsty person to use (in days when no one worried about germs). A primitive gravity flow system of lead pipes carried this water to Bay Avenue and Valley Street, where it flowed into another trough affording good spring water for people and horses. Schoolboys made pocket money by delivering water to homes in 10-gallon cans, following routes as boys in other towns did with newspapers. Other sources of freshwater from the hillside are along Bayside Drive in the Water Witch section, at 233 Shore Drive, and at the end of Spring Street.

The first 1907 borough water plant on Miller Street took water from an artesian well going more than 700 feet deep into the vast freshwater aquifer lying beneath Sandy Hook Bay, using a coal-fired steam pump. An improved 1948 plant took water from a new 714-foot-deep well pumped with electricity and delivering 550 gallons per minute at 110 pounds pressure.

Unfortunately, the water from the borough system was not without problems, which plagued the governing body for almost a century. The pumping apparatus switched between being steam driven and fired by coal at one time to oil at another time or electricity. Frequently, the piping had to be replaced, or withdrawn and cleaned and refitted. More than one well had to be driven to supply sufficient water or enough of a satisfactory quality, and at times, water even had to be borrowed from Atlantic Highlands. Then, there was the perennial problem of not enough water pressure, especially to supply the needs of homes and firetrucks fighting fires in the hillsides.

Besides all this, the borough had to keep and manage a team of water supply workers ("watermen," but of a different sort) with trucks and equipment and clerical staff to keep records and bills. The system often proved inefficient, especially considering the fact that not all homes and businesses in Highlands had water meters. Those that did have meters paid according to their usage; those that did not were charged an estimated annual charge. The inequity plagued the administration and set neighbor against neighbor. The resolution to the municipal water problem came when the water workers were dismissed and the whole system was approved by voters to be sold to the New Jersey American Water Company in November 1993 for $3,000,000.

As progress continued toward building the town's resources, businessmen united to do their part, and Highlands' first board of trade (the forerunner of today's chamber of

The first borough headquarters was Firemen's Hall at Bay and Valley and was purchased for $4,500 in 1910; later offices were located in a storefront at 171 Bay Avenue until the present Highlands Borough Hall was constructed in 1961.

Born in 1875, Jesse Sculthorp, a visionary entrepreneur and real estate developer, served as the borough's clerk for several years in the early part of the twentieth century.

commerce and Highlands Business Partnership) was formed June 1907 by Dr. John Opfermann, Addison Romain, George W. Hardy, and 42 other members in order to improve borough conditions and thereby business opportunities. It was re-organized in June 1912 under E.A. Intemann with renewed ambition and hope for an improved town. One of the first acts of the business organization, typical of all its projects throughout its existence, was to raise $350, matched by the borough's $350 to pave Bay Avenue with gravel. Later, they bought a street-spraying wagon to put "Dustolene" or water on the dirt streets to keep the dust down in hot, dry summer periods.

One sure sign of municipal progress was the April 20, 1910 voters' decision to raise $4,500 through a bond sale to permit the borough's purchase of Firemen's Hall on the corner of Bay and Valley Avenues to serve as Borough Hall and the police and fire department headquarters. Prior to this, mayor and council met in the large room on the second floor of Firemen's Hall, which was rented from the fire companies, and the borough clerk and recorder would keep official records at home. In July 1903, Borough Clerk Jesse Sculthorpe received, for the first time, a desk, file cabinet, and safe (at a cost of $40) for use in his home, where the March 17, 1903 council re-organization meeting was held. Things could be done rather informally back then, long before our "Sunshine Law" mandating business be conducted open to the public. In October 1925, council approved spending $7,000 to renovate the rear garage and jail and the general clean-up of Borough Hall. During the 1930s, Borough Hall moved across and down the street to a new hall, converted from a storefront located at 171 Bay Avenue; the fire, first aid, and police remained at the old site. When Hurricane Donna furiously lashed Highlands with wind, rain, and floods on September 12, 1960, they had to abandon Borough Hall and

Camping at Water Witch Station
Highlands, N. J.

This rare view of the inside of a camp site c. 1910 in the Water Witch section reveals the summer vacation conditions, the best affordable, of hard-working families escaping the heat, dirt, and crowds of places like Newark, Jersey City, Brooklyn, and Manhattan.

move to the Community Center, located near the water-pumping station on Miller Street. On December 5 that year, council resolved to demolish the old hall, add some adjacent property, and build a new Borough Hall and fire department headquarters on the same location. The first aid squad was then already in its own building on Valley Street. The present borough office building, fire department, and police station, costing $90,000, was dedicated on October 8, 1961.

Shortly after the borough administration moved into Borough Hall, council granted the Atlantic Highlands Gas Company a franchise on May 4, 1910, to pipe gas into town, and most of the work was quickly completed by mid-summer to meet the demand of the rapidly expanding business and residential areas of town.

Highlands' typical popularity for summer vacationers peaked the summer of 1910, when one day, the tourist population hit 20,000 people living in tents, houseboats, bungalows, cottages, boarding houses, and hotels or making day trips on the steamboats and trains from the cities to the north. Over 30,000 postcards were bought and mailed from the Highlands post office in just one weekend!

Highlands' Businessmen's Carnival of September 1, 2, and 3, 1910, celebrated both the town's business success and the tenth anniversary of the Borough of Highlands, the first of festivities to follow celebrating 50, 75, and 100 years of progress.

The excitement, popularity, and fame of Highlands and the area in summer was a natural draw also for the pioneer filmmakers such as Edison, Dickson, and the great D.W. Griffith, who began making movies in Highlands. In the early days of movie making, long before the discovery of Hollywood's benefits, when the fledgling filmmaking industry was still nested in New York, legendary pioneers of cinema came to New Jersey to shoot their films.

They crossed the Hudson once they realized their art was limited by indoor studio and stage sets, and came to New Jersey's undeveloped rural areas to shoot films requiring barren mountain crags and cliffs (the Palisades), or cowboy Western looks (Fort Lee), or desolate tropical islands, sands, and beaches (Highlands and Sea Bright). They went where transportation to the sets was fast, easy, and cheap, via subway, bus, and steamboat, rarely by automobile in the early days and thus they came to Highlands.

The American Mutoscope Company shot "Projectile from Ten Inch Disappearing Gun Striking Water, Sandy Hook" at the Proving Grounds at Fort Hancock in 1897 and "Spanish Battleship *Viscaya*" off Sandy Hook in February 1898. Thomas Edison's Vitascope Company shot "Start of the Ocean Race for the Kaiser's Cup" in May 1905 off Sandy Hook, "Ice Boat Racing on the North Shrewsbury" in Red Bank in 1904, and "Ten Pickaninnies" in August 1908 also in Red Bank.

The great innovative motion picture director D.W. Griffith and the equally talented camera operator G.W. "Billy" Bitzer came with their Biograph Company actors to Highlands and the nearby ocean beaches to shoot *After Many Years* (1908), with Linda Arvidson, who later became Mrs. Griffith; *Lines of White on a Sullen Sea* (October 28, 1909); *A Salutary Lesson*, with Mack Sennet and Linda Arvidson (August 11, 1910); and *The Sorrows of the Unfaithful*, with Mary Pickford (August 22, 1910).

During these early days of the moving pictures, the people in Highlands were already thoroughly enthralled with the entertainment miracles they witnessed on the silent screen in more than a half dozen picture houses in town. They, like movie enthusiasts everywhere, were beginning to recognize and follow from film to film the actors and actresses they met, even though they did not know their names, since production companies had not yet added credits to their films.

The first Highlands moving picture parlors were not real theaters or even permanent structures, but stores and open lots quickly set up for the entertainment fad. The first permanent theatre or auditorium devoted exclusively to stage and motion picture

The Marshall House was one of the many popular boarding houses on Navesink Avenue.

entertainment (surviving today at 78 Bay Avenue) was built in May 1909, and at first, was called Harry L. Sculthorpe's Auditorium, later "the Auditorium" or "Highlands Auditorium." The *Register* recorded an interesting incident on June 9, 1909:

> The auditorium draws big crowds of lovers of moving pictures. On Sunday night previous to Decoration Day, there was a full house. . . . It was found that the machine [the projector] had been tampered with and would not work. A discharged employee put the machine out of business. The audience got their money back [10¢].

Watching movies outside under the stars at night had its advantages in the days prior to air conditioning, and almost every town had its airdrome, or outside summer theater. Highland Beach had a large one adjacent to the Bamboo Garden in the 1920s. Summer tent and bungalow colonies such as the one at Gravelly Point showed films right on the beach (and still does today, especially for the kids).

As the art of motion picture writing, photography, direction, acting, and production matured through the 1920s, so did the showing of films. Temporary storefront venues gave way to permanent theaters. The Highlands Auditorium Theatre became the only place for moving picture entertainment in town and remained thus until the early 1920s. When the New Auditorium Theatre was built at 88 Bay Avenue around 1922, the old auditorium became the "Auditorium Garage," a function it still serves today. Although the actual opening date of the theater is yet to be determined, it is probable that the Highlands theater was built not long after the one in neighboring Atlantic Highlands, where the Atlantic Theatre's manager, Harry Kridel, threw open the doors on May 21, 1921, to a capacity crowd of 900 persons with some 200 disappointed people left waiting outside. The first film shown was *Sentimental Tommy*, with Gareth Hughes and an all-star cast.

Seen here c. 1912, the Highlands Auditorium was owned and operated by Harry Sculthorp.

In Highlands, the residents and tourists in town turned out in huge numbers to the Auditorium Theatre on September 3, 1927 to see Paramount's *Swim Girl, Swim,* starring Bebe Daniels, Josephine Dunn, James Hall, and Gertrude Ederle, who had just the summer before won worldwide fame and Highlands' hearts after becoming the first American and the first woman to swim across the English Channel on August 6, 1926.

In 1931, the Highlands Auditorium, which had changed ownership at least twice since its start, opened under new management as Tony Hunting's "Hunting Auditorium." He also owned the theater in Atlantic Highlands and ran it as "Tony Hunting's Atlantic Theatre." Hunting was an aggressive businessman and entrepreneur who in July 1931 began making his own movies of people and places about town, which he would show between feature films in order to attract residents and tourists who yearned to see themselves on the silver screen.

That same summer, professional cinematographers returned to shoot a film in the Highlands, the first since 1910, when D.W. Griffith was in town. Now it was Daniel Dorn of Red Bank who came to shoot his *Romance in Highlands,* starring Joe Dempsey as the Handsome Hero and Florence Dittes as the Beautiful Girl, which he rescues. Dempsey was the star and hero with leading lady, Florence Dittes, and his sister, Helen, in a supporting role, produced by Daniel Dorn Sr. and Daniel Dorn Jr. of Red Bank. It featured various activities and locations about town, such as the First Aid Squad's rescue and resuscitation of Mayor Hardy's son, Leonard, from a water death, while focusing on the falling in love and courtship of the beautiful, young couple. It was shown only locally in the Highlands Auditorium Theatre for three days (August 17–19) that summer for 50¢ admission. Afterwards, the Dorns gave the three reels of film to Mayor Hardy for safekeeping to be viewed by future generations to witness Highlands progress. Its location today is unknown and is presumed lost.

The theater in Highlands became the Marine Theatre, open only for the summer season when the crowds were in town, and was run in close conjunction with the Atlantic in Atlantic Highlands and the Casino in Keansburg during the 1950s and 1960s.

During the 1910s, Highlands was growing and was more and more becoming a very desirable place to live and to conduct business. In March 1914, Highlands doubled in size to its present dimension of .64 square mile when the Borough annexed all of Water Witch (except Monmouth Hills) and lands along Portland Road from Hillside Avenue to today's Hartshorne Woods by another act of the New Jersey Legislature, which approved it by a single vote margin. Much of the town's progress was due to its hard-working people, a real community dedicated to a better Highlands.

Nowhere is the town's spirit better seen than in the "Little Church built on fellowship." A miracle of community spirit and cooperation was witnessed in Highlands on October 28, 1914, when the cornerstone was laid in St. Andrew the Apostle Episcopal Church on Bay Avenue. People spoke about how the new church building was being constructed in the manner of the early Christian believers. People from all walks of life, from various economic backgrounds and differing attitudes toward religion, were united in a way rarely encountered now today or even back then. Some who could afford it donated money, but more important, all donated their time, talents, and hard work. Rich and poor, young and old, men, women, and children, even the vicar himself, Reverend Crawford, labored with

The Episcopal Church of St. Andrew the Apostle was originally built as a parish and community hall in 1914.

saws and trowels, with lumber and cement, in "building a people's house." They worked not for money, but for the feeling of great inner satisfaction in constructing St. Andrew's first new building.

Before this time, the church, incorporated February 9, 1906, was under the guidance of the Reverend John C. Lord, pastor of All Saints Memorial Episcopal Church, when St. Andrew's purchased the old Dutch Reformed Church, located at Fifth and Valley Streets. This had been the very first church established in Highlands, pastored by the Reverend Abraham Allen, who came to town in 1875 and built a small church, vicarage, and burial ground for his congregation. After Allen's death, the church went into such decline that it was sold to the Episcopalians, with the few remaining Reformed Church members joining St. Andrew's.

Once the remains in some dozen graves were removed and reinterred at All Saints cemetery in 1914, property on Bay Avenue was bought, and a few years later, the little old church building on Fifth Street was sold and moved to Bay Avenue to become Cohen's Market.

The building being constructed actually was originally conceived to be a parish hall for church functions as well as for community and borough affairs, a "people's house," for public meeting space was critically lacking in Highlands Borough at that time. Architect and supervisor of the building was L.J. Aimer of Navesink, described by people as a "live wire" and responsible for keeping the volunteer workforce charged up. William Wells from Atlantic Highlands was the general contractor. Both these men also volunteered many hours of effort beyond their contracted agreement.

Two celebrities took part in the work as well. Robert Hartshorne, a parishioner of All Saints Church, donated a vast quantity of lumber that was taken from the "Hartshorne Woods" and milled by his employees on his farm. William Barclay Parsons, an area summer resident, volunteered his world-renowned engineering experience. He had built the first New York City subway, the Cape Cod Canal, and participated on the Panama Canal.

Plans to build a real church attached to the front side of the parish hall and thus creating a cross in the form of the letter T, unfortunately, never were realized due to economic hardship in the less than affluent Highlands community of the 1920s. The parish then made the best of the situation and renovated the hall on the first floor into a beautiful and well-appointed chapel that was functional as well as warm, inviting, and inspirational for the congregation's worshippers.

The number of faithful so dwindled in recent years that the Episcopal bishop of New Jersey directed the closing of the church and the last Episcopal service was held under Pastor Margaret Coffey on St. Andrew's feast day, 2000. Afterwards, the church was sold. Today, Reverend Martin McGrail is pastor of St. Andrew Christian Church, which holds open its doors for nondenominational worship services and for community social and welfare programs.

To those who do not know well the character of the people of Highlands, such town-wide activity must seem extraordinary and remarkable. While it is indeed so, it is also quite typical of Highlanders, from the earliest times right up to the present, for given a cause in which they believe, the people will work for the joy of service to others in need.

Summer in Highlands at this time was not just for the out-of-town tourists and summer-people, for the regular Highlanders, young and old alike, took advantage of the season to play or watch the game of baseball. What happened on the Highlands diamond affected the game of baseball worldwide. Today, baseball is played and followed enthusiastically in Japan, and American teams are starting to use Japanese players, thanks, in part, to the energies of a Highlands man and his love for the "American game." "America's Baseball Ambassador to Japan," as sportswriters later proclaimed him, was

The Highland Stars pose for this c. 1911 portrait after playing ball on their homemade diamond on the Kay and Cornwall property.

Herbert Harrison Hunter fields a ball at second base for the New York Giants c. 1917. He went on to introduce the American game to Japan.

Herbert Harrison Hunter, who received his training in baseball and fell in love with the game on the sandlot built by a team called the Stars in the summer of 1910 on property not far from the Shrewsbury River.

Playing for the Stars and two other Highlands teams, the Oasis and the Melrose, against clubs from as far away as Newark, Hunter was known as a savage left-handed batter and a versatile fielder. Despite his competitiveness, he was considered such a fair person that even at age 16, he served as umpire when necessary.

The New York Giants had great expectations for Hunter and in June 1916 signed him to come immediately play third base against Pittsburgh. It was an inauspicious beginning, for the first game went badly for Hunter, who got spiked so viciously by the Pirates Jimmy Johnson that he was disabled for the next few games. They traded him to the Chicago Cubs, who then sold him off in 1917 to the San Francisco Seals, a minor league club. Hunter returned to the majors in 1920 to play outfield for the Boston Red Sox, and in 1921, for the St. Louis Cardinals. After just 39 games in four brief seasons, his time in the majors was finished. Hunter's real career would be elsewhere.

While with the Seals, he was introduced to many university students from Japan with little skill but with great zeal for the game of baseball he loved so much. He saw the great potential for the game in Japan and resolved to bring it there. On his first trip to Japan at the end of the 1921 season, Hunter brought a small exhibition team and stayed on to coach ball teams for Keio and Waseda Universities. He was popular with the Japanese and showed so much managerial skill to players in America that in the 1922–1923 off-season, he brought to Japan, Korea, and the Philippines, players from both the National and American League champions: Emil Meusel, George Kelly, and Casey Stengel of the Giants and Waite Hoyt, Joe Bush, and Herb Pennock of the Yankees. Press releases from the tour showed Hunter "arm-in-arm for baseball" with Japanese players who were quoted as saying, "As long as Japan and the United States have something in common like baseball, there is bound to exist nothing but the best of relations." The Americans said, "On the diamond, a peace is being made that politicians cannot break."

During the 1920s, Hunter went to Japan eight times coaching at universities there. In 1929, he brought Freddy Hoffmann, Bob Shawkey, and the great Ty Cobb to assist with training, and they wore the uniforms of the host teams. The pinnacle of Hunter's Japanese success came in 1931, when he brought 23 of the best Major League players on tour of the biggest Japanese universities. They played 17 games, at which the average paid attendance was 30,000 fans.

In 1932, a Japanese team came to play in Princeton and Yale, sponsored by Hunter, who had them stop off at the old ballfield of the Highlands–Atlantic Highlands Stars, located in Atlantic Highlands at the area of Columbia and Many Mind Avenues, for a fun demonstration game at which both Hunter and Babe Ruth played against the Japanese boys of summer. Today in Japan, baseball, with two leagues, Central and Pacific, each with six teams, is the national sport second only to sumo wrestling thanks to Herbert Harrison Hunter, a boy from Highlands.

For the next several years, life in Highlands was quiet, especially each September through June, once all the summer crowds had gone. While Highlands was quiet, people followed in the newspapers the disquieting events over in Europe, where what they called the "World War," or "the Great War," was raging and causing turmoil in the hearts of mothers and wives of boys and men. More and more, Highlands men were finding good paying work over on Sandy Hook's Fort Hancock and the U.S. Proving Grounds. For some time, just prior to America's entry into the war, Highlanders noticed the growing number of military freight trains coming through town for the fort. Businesses noted the increase of soldiers stationed on the fort who came into town for recreation. However, some were resented when they caused trouble in the bars or with the local girls, but most were welcomed for the money they spent.

A "welcome home" celebration was held on Saturday, September 12, 1919, when the soldiers and sailors of Highlands came back from the Great World War. Stores and

A "Welcome Home" celebration was held for World War I soldiers on September 12, 1919.

businesses, decorated in American bunting, closed at noon. Down Bay Avenue, the main street, 60 veterans were led by Captain James J. Rowland, M.D., on horseback, with Mayor Fred Kieferdorf and council and clergy following in automobiles. Thirty decorated autos and trucks were in the parade. Schoolchildren, Boy Scouts, and Girl Scouts were in the line of march. The people cheered on the sidelines for the grand parade. When the parade dispersed, the band went to three homes where men who lost their lives in the Great War used to live. They played "Nearer, my God, to Thee" before each home and marched away in sad silence.

The people in Highlands, like people everywhere, sent boys away to war and welcomed back men. They too lost boys who would never become men. A memorial was needed to remind them of the sacrifices of these veterans. Towns all along the bay and rivers were planning their monuments that year. But in Highlands, it took six years to raise the $4,000 necessary for a fitting tribute. A monument committee each year raised funds by soliciting donations, running dances and card parties, showing movies, and holding theatrical shows. Finally, a monument was erected—the statue of an American doughboy, carved in stone, standing 6 feet tall upon a granite base 20 feet high. It was unveiled at the 11th hour, on the 11th day, of the 11th month, Armistice Day of 1924, now our Veterans' Day.

Almost every person in Highlands came out for the dedication and parade down Navesink Avenue (Route 36) to the spot just before the present bridge, called East View Hill. Here, they spoke of the contributions of all the veterans—of the Civil War, of the Spanish-American War, and of the World War. Finally, after all the speeches and the formal words and invocations and benedictions, after the bands from Fort Hancock played and

Originally, this monument was dedicated on Armistice Day, November 11, 1924, to men who served in the Civil War, the Spanish-American War, and the World War, but it stands today in tribute to service men and women of later wars in Europe, the Pacific, Vietnam, and the Middle East. The doughboy of World War I atop the monument keeps watch, gazing toward France in the east, looking for his comrades who did not return home.

Highlands Methodist Episcopal Church, built in 1908 under Reverend Thomas Hess, received the Victory Clock in 1922, a memorial to veterans of World War I as a result of contributions during the days of Prohibition.

the local fire companies sang, after the leaders of the Daughters of Liberty displayed their banners, finally the American flag, which draped the statue, was removed. The band play the "Star-Spangled Banner" and they cheered, they prayed, they wept, and they remembered. The doughboy still stands there today, much as he has from the beginning, despite a damaged helmet and slight adjustments to accommodate the new bridge of 1932. He has stood as a memorial for men and women in later wars in Europe, the Pacific, in Korea, in Vietnam, and in the Middle East. The soldier stands tall and silent, his gaze fixed straight out to the eastern horizon, pointing towards France, as if looking and waiting for the five comrades who never came home. A bronze plaque speaks for him and the people of Highlands, "Veterans, we will never forget."

A more subtle memorial of the struggle made by the men of Highlands during the great World War, or World War I by today's standards, came to be called the Victory Clock. It was not until 1922 that the tower of the Methodist church on Bay Avenue had a clock, having stood some 12 years with a large round hole where a clock should be. The Victory Clock was paid for by the people of Highlands, but in a novel manner. Mayor "Bud" Bahrs remembered that during Prohibition, the pastor of the church each Monday would walk down Bay Avenue stopping at all the many places he knew alcohol was being illegally supplied and consumed through the efforts of local rum runners. He would place his hat on a table and visit each local patron of the establishment to offer instruction if desired. Typically, he would respectfully have no converts but would find a hat full of dollars as he departed. Soon, there was enough money to complete the church tower with a Victory Clock.

That same autumn of patriotism and pomp, on September 15, 1924, the Joshua Huddy monument to the hero-martyr of the Revolution was rededicated in an elaborate ceremony. The monument was originally situated on the southeast side of Water Witch Avenue some 125 feet from the railroad tracks, the actual spot where the tree once stood from which he was hanged by pro-British forces. The unity exhibited in patriotic demonstrations like these and so characteristic of people during the first quarter century of the Borough of Highlands was starting to weaken. During the tenure of Mayor Fred Kieferdorf in 1920, tensions surfaced between the sections of town when the residents in the hills demanded the right to start their on fire department. The mayor was correct in his interpretation of the reasons behind the request and was firm in his refusal, in his persuasion that Highlands was one town in which all people must learn to work with and for each other and to lay aside insignificant differences. Problems were surfacing again, problems caused by Highlands' "split personality."

Today, Highlands is a town built on two geographic levels, commonly called lower Highlands and upper Highlands, at sea level or just slightly above and at an elevation from 75 to 240 feet, respectively. The two levels of terrain have become synonymous, over time, with two economic levels as well. Animosity and distrust have developed also over the years, and unflattering and undeserved labels have been used for residents in the two areas. People in the lower part of town have been called "clammeys," or "clam diggers," while those in the upper ranges have been known as "goat-hillers."

In the nineteenth century, the split could be attributed to differences of background and religion. In the first influx of immigrants to town came Irish Catholics, arriving in growing numbers after the Civil War through about 1920. They settled separate from the "native" folk, who were generally Protestant fishermen and clammers on the low, flat, and sandy lands below. They lived in the hillsides, unified as Catholics and identified by accent and name, around the church of Our Lady of Perpetual Help. They worked as farmhands, gardeners, telegraphers, trainmen, and servants.

In one nearby part of the hills over on Portland Road and along Navesink Avenue, actors and theatrical families from New York built palatial-looking "cottages" in which to pass the summer's heat and which put their affluence on display. In another part of the hills, Water Witch Club members appeared much the same to Highlanders on the streets adjoining Bay Avenue below.

Initially there was very little weakening of the forces of separation as can be seen from the names of elected officials and firemen in the early decade of the borough. The early summer tourists came to lower Highlands attractions to spend their money, to live in hotels there or on the hill, and then leave after a day, weekend, week, or season. Some of these visitors verbalized their distaste for and to the lower Highlanders they encountered, resulting in fistfights at times.

Despite many people of several various ethnic immigrant backgrounds (Irish, Jews, Germans, Poles, Italians, etc.) coming and settling in Highlands during the period between the two world wars, they tended to find homes and open shops in downtown Highlands, rather than up in the hills. Despite all Highlands children being educated in basic American values in the same elementary school (up on the hill), the prejudices did not diminish significantly.

Matters, in fact, intensified in the post war years of the 1950s and 1960s when economic depression and blight, caused by several factors, overwhelmed the lower town, being characterized by urban renewal, government-financed low-income housing, and trailer parks. Upper Highlands appeared untouched. In recent years, many public-spirited individuals and groups of residents and businessmen have done much in conjunction with the borough's elected and appointed officials and schoolteachers to make noticeable improvements to the image of Highlands both in reality and in the minds of outsiders.

The split, although somewhat mitigated, still exists, nonetheless, for there are many people today in lower town whose children will not or must not visit upper children's homes to play and hang out, and there are people who never go downtown, except to a restaurant by car, and there are persons who only go down to buy a lottery ticket and a newspaper and otherwise would not know Central Avenue from Center Street or John Street from Matthews Street. The division, of course, is an expression of prejudice on both sides. Yet, the prejudice of anti-Semitism appears not to have found overt expression, by way of contrast, to the credit of the people. Jews seem to have been accepted and involved in Highlands affairs from the start. Bendet Rosenblum, a Jew, was an important proponent of Highlands Borough and signed the inaugurating petition in 1900. He was a founding member of the Seaside Fire Department and in 1928 was honored as marshal of the Firemen's Parade and Party, dressed in his original red, white, and blue uniform. He and his partner, Sam Silberblatt, ran a dry goods store on Bay Avenue for many years and served the community on the board of education for almost as long. Rosenblum's application for American citizenship, on file in the Monmouth County Archives, includes

This c. 1907 photograph shows Highlands Hills and the two different levels of terrain in the community.

Bill and Joel Kendrick are pictured here loading a basket of clams during the winter in Highlands.

a letter of character reference written by longtime Highlander Lewis Parker. It was Rosenblum who established on Navesink Avenue in the old DuVale house off Miller Street a summer home for poor Jewish children from the cities during the late 1920s and early 1930s.

Black people, however, have not fared so well, unfortunately, in Highlands during most of its history, although attitudes have ameliorated somewhat in the past few years as a small number of black families have come into town. The first "colored" people in Highlands came well before 1900 and until about 1920 to live and work in the large hotels along the river and near the bridge during the summers only. Thanks to the census registers, today's researcher can find out their names, ages, and places of birth. The *Highlands Star–Atlantic Highlands Journal* tells one nothing about the black experience or the overall relations of blacks and whites in Highlands.

Troubles of another kind developed for the large number of Highlands men who depended on clamming to support their families. In January 1925, New York City officials placed an embargo on clams taken from the rivers and Sandy Hook Bay around Highlands due to suspected illness in persons eating clams taken from the local waters contaminated with pollution from untreated sewerage. At first, the ban was lifted on February 11, that year, only to return April 15, 1926, to be more vigorously enforced for the next ten years until finally being lifted on October 15, 1935. Faced with loss of the vital New York market, Highlands clammers struggled, despite the clam bonanza discovered in waters near town in the early 1930s, which supplied money from seed clams for Virginia and markets not in the city. Their troubles made the watermen glad they had formed their Protective Association back on November 1, 1905, and had purchased for $1,600 their "Association Lot" off Fifth Street for boat storage and repair. Clammers did not generally earn much; at this time, a man clearing brush at the Twin Lights was paid $3.40 per day and clammers earned considerably less.

It is no wonder many of the town's watermen adapted their boating skills to more profitable work on the local waters, making Highlands a hub in the rumrunning era. This account of the days rumrunners evaded authorities in and around Highlands to satisfy their customers' desires and to better their own financial gain all in the face of the Prohibition laws is based on newspaper reports and on the personal reminiscences shared by John "Buddy" Bahrs, former mayor, restaurateur, Highlands native, but not "rumrunner."

Bahrs was just a 12-year-old boy when Prohibition became the law nationwide on January 20, 1920. His father had been taking the family from their home in Newark to Highlands to spend the summer since 1912 and one summer found what he considered a great opportunity, buying a boathouse and boat rental business located on the river at the foot of Cedar Street where the James T. White Clam Depuration Plant stands today. Later, his father, John H. Bahrs, and mother, Florence, bought McGuire's boathouse on the site of today's Bahrs Landing Restaurant, where the whole family moved in. It was a tough life for the mother and kids living year-round in the two-story boathouse that had a half-dozen bunks on one floor and some 50 on the other, all with mattresses stuffed with cornstalks and straw. Soon weekend fishermen made Bahrs their headquarters and the kids, Ruth, Al, Ken, and Buddy, sleeping on the hard and cold bunks, made it their home, without ever a complaint. Fishermen used to pay $3.50 each for boat, bait, bunk, and board provided by Florence Bahrs's good home cooking, which was served on tables covered with sheet metal. There were no menus, no tablecloths or napkins, and no complaints, just thanks from the fishermen going for flounder, fluke, porgies, and stripped bass in the river.

The rumrunners, or bootleggers, made Highlands their base of illegal operations since it was the nearest New Jersey town to the offshore supply ships and since there were

This more contemporary scene of Highlands shows Bahrs Restaurant, a location where many rumrunners gathered to find food and shelter.

plenty of large, powerful, and fast-moving lobster boats (refitted with very powerful war surplus airplane engines) there for easy hire to bring the whiskey contraband around the Hook and into waiting cars and trucks, having outrun any pursuing Coast Guard patrol boats. They chose Bahrs because it was right on the water, close to the ocean, and offered warm hospitality, decent accommodations, and good food, especially Florence's clam chowder.

While the buyers were all men from the cities with associations to a tougher criminal element in organized crime, the men who ran the boats were all locals, good seamen, hard-working lobstermen, and clammers who saw nothing wrong with their participation in this victimless crime, who struggled to make ends meet even before the Depression hit, and who were legitimized in their unlawfulness by the senselessness of the law that no one ever wanted, that no one respected. These Highlands men would ride out past the 3-mile limit of U.S. jurisdiction, day or night, in storm or calm, to "rum row" off Highlands, Sea Bright, Monmouth Beach, and Long Branch, where a small fleet of ships from Canada awaited boats carrying buyers.

At first, rumrunning boats operated in broad daylight since initially there was no patrol set up to stop them. However, soon they had to work under the cover of darkness to disguise their crime a bit. The city men would sit around one or more iron stoves in Bahrs, talking, playing cards, even reading, and always waiting to find out when and where the boats were coming in with their purchases. A lookout on the rocks over at Highland Beach used binoculars and a powerful flashlight to detect and respond to prearranged signals from the boats at "rum row"; then shining his beams into Bahrs, he let the men know where to meet the boats, at Highlands, in Leonardo, in Belford, or someplace else. All the men jumped up, downed their drinks or coffees, and ran to their cars and trucks. They used big and fast Diamond Reo Speed Wagons, but many preferred long sedans

This local Highlands crew loads a sailing vessel with cases of Canadian whiskey or Jamaican rum from a ship anchored off the coast during the days of Prohibition.

fitted up with extra heavy-duty springs, since these had the needed space, the speed, and the element of disguise. With 15 or more cases of Canadian whiskey in the backs of the cars, they would ride to the city looking just like plain, ordinary people returning from the shore.

The bootleggers who worked through Bahrs—Whitey, Dutch, Providence, and Dingbat were some of the aliases used—respected the family and its business, were polite especially to Mrs. Bahrs, treated the kids well, and always paid their bills with generosity. However, the respect was not necessarily reciprocated. John Bahrs knew full well what he was doing was wrong, but it was business and times were tough as he was just starting out and he had to make a living and feed his family. Many a local and many a bootlegger thought Bahrs should use his large sea skiff for a more lucrative business than the pound-net fishing it had been built for by Seaman Boats in Long Branch. They urged Jack Bahrs to get with it, to wise up, and to take the boat out and load it up with whiskey, to make a real dollar or two. He hated what he was already doing. His good wife, Florence, worried about the whole affair and wanted no part of it, so he refused.

It seemed that everyone was into the bootlegging affair, including the officer-in-charge at the Coast Guard base on Sandy Hook, who would get a telephone call that rum boats were coming into Highlands. He would send his patrol and gun boats to look in a different location, say, by Perth Amboy. The men would find nothing, but he would find a quarter case of good Canadian waiting on the dock. Just about everyone in Highlands reaped the benefits of Prohibition and rumrunning. They made plenty of fast money and spent it swiftly. The women who worked in the clam shucking and stringing sheds along the river suddenly had fur coats to keep them warm in the bitterly cold huts and homes. Some even glamorously displayed new diamond rings on their fingers, like the movie starlets they saw, fingers like stubs from opening clams.

From time to time there would be raids on Highlands speakeasies. Police would swoop into several places simultaneously and the results would be read in the papers the next Thursday—not in the *Star* or the *Journal*, the local town papers—in the *Red Bank Register*; for example, on June 11, 1930, the paper carried the following story: "County detectives made five raids at the Highlands. The owners of the places were arraigned in Freehold and held in $1,000 bail for the Grand Jury on charges of illegal possession and sale. Arrested were Tom C——, Emil A——, S. W——, Michael M——, and Frank M——." Apparently, it was without public shame or disapproval that they remained in town, using their profits to finance memorial windows in the new church being built and opening legal taverns after Prohibition was over.

The glamour evaporated, the money devalued, the thrills vanished, whenever a bootlegging affair went contrary to expectations and Coast Guard machine gun bullets ripped open a man's spine in a boat headed for shore and he died sprawled on the floor of the sedan intended for whiskey, or a man was blinded for life in an explosion, pouring naphtha instead of gasoline into a hot boat engine to make it run faster when being pursued. When the 21st Amendment to the Constitution repealed the 18th Amendment, national Prohibition came to an end on December 5, 1933. The lobstermen returned to their lobster pots, the clammers to their boats, bushels, and rakes, and people returned to the 26 taverns licensed in the little borough just .64 square mile.

The Highland House, seen here c. 1910, was built in 1898 and was destroyed in a 1927 fire. It was one of the four grand hotels on Navesink Avenue near the bridge.

The Borough of Highlands began March 22, 1900; however, the development of the town, aside from the annexation of the Water Witch section and some land along Portland Road south of Hillside Avenue, owed little to the form of government in place during this phase.

Responding to the beginning tourist crunch, four new hotels were built or expanded, three at the end of Navesink Avenue (south side) closest to the bridge, the Victoria, the Monmouth House (1903), and the Highland House (1898) (left to right looking from across the street), and one, the Martin House (1906), at Portland Road and Highland Avenue. A bit farther from the river on the opposite side of Navesink Avenue came the Leonard House (*c.* 1908) and the Marshall House (*c.* 1909). In lower Highlands things were moving just as rapidly with the brick Creighton Hotel (1906 or 1907; later called Kruse's Pavilion) on Bay Avenue (today's Number 24), the Seaside Hotel (1901) at the northeast corner of Miller Street and Bay Avenue, the Bieber Cottage Hotel (*c.* 1908), the Cedar Grove Hotel of William Conners (1907) in the Water Witch part of town, and other smaller places of accommodation.

At approximately the same period, tent and/or bungalow colonies began to appear all over, such as the Chris Williams Cottages (1908), Cashion's grove, and Tom McGuinness's grove, all located in or near today's Veterans' Park on Bay Avenue and at Conners and Gravelly Point.

The push for lots prompted development of the Kay and Cornwell tract and the laying in of streets and laying out lots, all after the low spots of standing water and swamp had been filled in with sand pumped from the nearby river bed, thus effectively creating land where none existed before. Kay, Cornwell, Jackson, Center, and John Streets and Shrewsbury Avenue became real estate opportunities that filled out with houses in the 1910s and 1920s.

On the other side of town, the Water Witch Development Company had been working since 1906 to attract summer or year-round residents to the area. The company had Asa E. Dennett as its marketing agent and F.B. Rogers as its contractor and builder. The brochure made the place sound irresistible:

> If you are looking for happiness and contentment, come to Water Witch . . . no other place like it on the Atlantic coast . . . no malaria, no mosquitoes . . . hills, river and ocean, good bathing and fishing . . . a settlement where everybody is congenial . . . terms so easy that most anybody can secure a home and prepare for old age. If your nerves are unstrung, come . . . and breathe the fresh and invigorating air which comes off the sea like a balm . . . within comfortable commutation reach of New York City and cities of northern New Jersey . . . one hundred trains a day, besides the Patten Line and Merchant Line steamers . . . very liberal terms, taking a small cash deposit and easy monthly payments, and to cash buyers a liberal discount.

The streets laid out were pleasures to build on, Water Witch Avenue, Snug Harbor Avenue, Washington, Huddy, Barberie, Seadrift, Atlantic; Cheerful, Recreation, and Marine Places—and Bay Avenue, of course. The deeds had some restrictions, which any

The Water Witch Casino, located at the end of the boat basin on Washington Avenue and Cheerful Place, was the social center of the quasi-autonomous Water Witch section of town.

117

"reasonable" lot buyer of the time would accept: one could not build a slaughterhouse or run a place of ill-repute, and one could not sell to Jews or Negroes—a common clause in many real estate contracts in primarily Protestant communities during this time period. By the late 1930s, hardly an empty lot remained despite the Depression.

Private clubs were everywhere, perhaps emulating the grand old clubs such as the Neptune, the Jackson, and the Water Witch Clubs, generally serving city people of similar backgrounds and locations. Some began as tent camps and quickly changed over to bungalow or cottage clubs. The names were mentioned in the newspapers, sometimes for the trouble they caused, but most often for some social event. There were Camp Harrison (both sides of Atlantic Street to the river), Camp Newark, the Newark Club, the Seaside Club, Lawrence Cottage, Honey Suckle Lodge, and Gravelly Point, to name just a few.

Several establishments like Conners and Gravelly Point, while open to the general public for weekly or full seasonal rentals of summer bungalows, became de facto clubs or associations, as the same families returned summer after summer to the same bungalows. Everyone watched out for each other's children; everyone knew his/her neighbors' names: Gravelly's Byrnes, Flood, Briody, McQuade, Mahoney, Jablonsky, Houston, and Herpich; Conners's McVickers, Bambury, Bode, Cassidy, Rooney, and Conlon, and then some. They were known as Conners and Gravelly families.

Prior to 1936, the neighborhood on Ocean Avenue, Beach Boulevard, and Central Avenue, as well as the borough recreation building, its beach, and parking lot, did not exist. As a matter of fact, Bay Avenue stopped just about at Snug Harbor Avenue. The whole area was a marsh that extended from the Water Witch bulkhead to Gravelly Point and from the river almost up to the CRRNJ tracks (today's Shore Drive). The entrance to Gravelly Point, Conners, and the two hotels beyond, the Greenland and the one which became today's Doris 'n' Ed's Restaurant, was via what was called the "back road," which

Seaside Club, Highlands, N. J.

This 1906 postcard shows members of the Seaside Club.

Dr. John L. Opfermann, a prominent local physician, served as the postmaster and the mayor of Highlands.

was a straight continuation of Bayside Drive to Water Witch Avenue along the base of the hill. In about 1936, the channel in the river was dredged and the sand was used to fill in the marsh, thus creating three streets and building lots where none had previously existed. Summer homes and Roxy's Boats (today formerly Long John's Restaurant and parking, now in 2001 the Highlands on the Bay Condominiums) soon appeared.

When Dr. John Opfermann began his second year as mayor in 1926, he summarized in a speech his estimate of the state of the Borough of Highlands. He emphasized that Highlands made most of its money from summer tourism and lamented the absence of factories or industries other than fishing to provide year-round income. He prioritized Highlands' needs as a sewer system, public beaches with free bathing, a large public fishing and boating pier, bathing pavilions like Highland Beach on Sandy Hook, concrete paving of Bay Avenue and Miller and Water Witch hills, water meters on every home and business rather than flat-rate fees, and adequate parking space for automobiles that entered town in ever-growing numbers. He took pleasure in announcing Highlands valuation as $2,500,000 and only $36,046.35 to be raised in taxes.

In Dr. Opfermann's last year and Dr. Rowland's following two years as mayor, Highlands got its sewer system, beaches and bathing pavilion, concrete street paving, some advances with water meters, plus a state-of-the-art garbage incinerator. However, no progress was made to establish an industrial base. The Business and Civic Organization and the newly formed Highlands Lions Club spent their resources promoting Highlands as a great summer resort. Even less could be done about automobile congestion and parking. During this time, the first reports were released by the New Jersey Highway Department regarding a new "super" highway 36 to run from Keyport to Highlands and a modern drawbridge to replace the old relic from 1892. Little did the Highlands leaders

119

The entire town of Highlands turned out for the "Welcome Home Trudy Ederle" parade on Bay Avenue. On August 6, 1926, Miss Ederle was the first American and the first woman to swim across the English Channel.

realize these would initiate a rapid and steady decline of tourists to town, who ultimately would race their automobiles right on past without even noticing its existence.

The summer of 1926 was a hot one and its August humidity was down right intolerable. Everyone moved more slowly and complained incessantly. They needed something to break the heat or at least take their minds off it. Relief came from Highlands summer resident Gertrude Ederle. Everyone knew her as Trudy and what Trudy had done was just amazing and brought them chills of excitement and pride to know that Highlander Gertrude Ederle at 3:25 p.m. Highlands time on August 6, 1926, became the first American, the first woman to swim across the English Channel, establishing a world-record achievement of swimming 35 miles in 14 hours, 30 minutes.

People were crying for joy, and they remembered her as just a little girl when her German-born father tied a rope around her waist, threw her off the dock into the swiftly moving Shrewsbury River steps from their bungalow, and yelled, "Swim, Trudy, swim!" Swim she did, and then kept on swimming amazing feats in the water. By age 18, she would capture 18 world records in distance swimming and win a gold medal and two bronzes at the 1924 Paris Olympics. Her achievements had taken Trudy Ederle to Europe and its capitals three times, to most every significant American city in the East, South, and Midwest, even to Hollywood to shoot a film called *Swim, Girl Swim*, reminiscent of her father's words her first time in the water. She met many of the other great athletes, celebrities, and journalists of the world, even dancing with the legendary Johnny Weismueller and having a song composed for her, "Trudy," by the great Irving Berlin. After the channel, she became, in the words of President Coolidge, "America's best girl," had a ticker-tape parade down Broadway, and a hometown parade down Navesink and Bay Avenues in Highlands. Throughout it all, always maintaining her characteristic humility, she said and still says today to friends with a twinkle in her eyes and musical lilt in her voice, "You know, my heart is in the Highlands."

When the stock market plunged on "Black Thursday," October 24, 1929, and brought the beginning of the Great Depression, hardly a Highlander noticed the economic chaos 26 miles across the water. While national unemployment would skyrocket to 25% in 1933 and the harms it brought would be compounded by the Revenue Act of 1932, which doubled income tax for most Americans, during the ten-year period of the Great Depression several events tended to alleviate somewhat the harsh economic times felt elsewhere for Highlands residents and summer visitors.

There were a number of indicators of apparent prosperity, despite the dark days of the Depression. The new New Jersey Route 36 stretched wide from Keyport to Highlands in 1932, often called the Boulevard, a prestigious sign of good times along the bay shore. It terminated in the award-winning so-called Million Dollar Bridge—imagine $1,000,000 in 1933—crossing the Shrewsbury River from Highlands to Sea Bright. On Monday, December 1, 1930, pupils and teachers of Highlands Elementary School, along the gleaming white concrete highway, started classes in the newly constructed school at Water Witch Avenue and a new church for Our Lady of Perpetual Help parish was built and consecrated in 1932.

Highlands got its own first aid squad at a time when volunteer squads were rare throughout New Jersey. It was organized in 1930, when six firemen received first aid

The Highlands–Sea Bright bridge, the award-winning "Million Dollar Bridge," is shown here in the first stages of construction as the huge concrete supports are being poured. The bridge was to be the culmination of the much acclaimed Highway 36, the "Queen of Roads," stretching some 12 miles from Keyport to Highlands.

The Dr. Mary Reed Maternity Hospital was located here at 254 Navesink Avenue from 1931 to 1935, providing modern medical care for local women.

training and certification. On March 11, 1931, the squad bought its first ambulance from Worden Funeral Home in Red Bank. On July 22, 1931, the Mary Reed Maternity Hospital opened at 254 Navesink Avenue to provide modern maternity and pre- and post-natal care for Highlands women. More than ten area physicians, including Highlands' own Doctors John Opfermann and James Rowland, attended patients here where several dozens of babies came into the world assisted by "Doctor" Mary Reed, herself a pioneer in the medical field at the time.

These were physical things Highlanders were proud to have in town. There were others things as well that made Depression life less depressing—for example, work. There was ample work available at Fort Hancock, on the construction of the highway, bridge, church, and school, although some two dozen Highlands men were caught in a job scam when they paid $25 each to a bogus employment agent who promised to get them good-paying jobs on the bridge work. When they showed up on the set day for work and there were no jobs, they knew they had been taken "for a ride" over the bridge. The clam bonanza discovered in Sandy Hook Bay in 1931 and the lifting of the New York City embargo in 1935 brought in large sums of cash to ease the times for many clamming families. The clam put food on the table, literally, for many a family, keeping parents and children well fed, especially with clam fritters. A new clothing factory for "dress goods" (Elias Sayour Co. of New York City) was opened October 17, 1935, on the site of the old elementary school, destroyed by fire in 1928, giving employment to 75 Highlands women at about $11 to $15.50 per week. Prior to this company, the failed Ever Ready Garment Co. had leased the building at the same rate of $500 per annum. Later, on March 14, 1946, Carmen Caruso bought the factory for $6,800 from the Borough (the sale was voided since the Borough did not own the property and was redone with the board of education) at the petition of 50 women from town. Roosevelt's WPA found the money to reconstruct the Water Witch bulkhead in November 1935, putting property owners at ease regarding floods and Highlands men to work on the project.

The life of people who were out of work and whose income was low or seasonal was made more pleasant by shopkeepers like John Azzolina. Highlands native Lilian Maxson recalled the following regarding what Azzolina did for people:

> He would trust you and he gave us credit. When we first asked for it, he would only allow us $2 and when he seen that we paid, then he gradually extended. And he did that for all the clammers. He once told me that in all the years he trusted the clammers he got stuck for less than $200. He was an Italian man, who came from Italy. He spoke broken English, but he had a heart of gold.

Another person worked tirelessly to help Highlanders and soon became a town legend in her own time. She was Jennie Parker, or Aunt Jennie, living in the heart of Parkertown at Fourth and Valley. She was something of a midwife, assisting Dr. Roland, Dr. Opfermann, or out-of-town physicians with deliveries at home, rarely delivering babies alone. For a week before birth, she would visit the mother each day preparing her breakfast and teaching her pre-natal health care. After the birth, she would visit daily,

The home of Jennie Parker, seen in this picture taken by town photographer Kyril Parker, still remains today after slight alteration and modernization at the corner of Fourth and Valley Streets.

making breakfast for the mother, sometimes preparing and leaving lunch as well, would help her wash herself and the baby, and would give basic baby care lessons as needed. Her bill would typically run no more than $20.

While all these were positive signs that Highlands was not so bad off in comparison with places like Kansas or Camden, there also were indicators of economic troubles for the town. For example, the steamboats stopped running in 1932. They stopped bringing city people to Highlands to spend their money, and the romantic *Mary Patten* and her sister boats were left to rot at the docks. The merchants reasoned all was not lost, for they still had the trains and automobiles to bring summer visitors. However, the new highway led increasing numbers of motorists, oblivious of the main street businesses in the lower section, right past Highlands. For property owners, it became really difficult. In May 1934, delinquencies were at $168,441 owed in taxes and $30,728 in water fees. By 1937, when the tax rate was forced up to $47.62 per $1,000 assessed value, Highlands residents were in trouble as was the borough, which was dependent on tax revenue from them. People stopped paying their taxes, their water fees, and their mortgages. The result was a massive

This c. 1955 photograph was taken south of the bridge from Sandy Hook and shows the Highlands hills and the bridge.

Civilian workers, perhaps Civilian Conservation Corps members, pose for this c. 1936 photograph in front of a 12-inch railroad mortar of Battery C, 52nd Coast Artillery in Fort Hancock.

number of foreclosures by the Highlands Building and Loan Association, the Atlantic Highlands B and L Association, the Atlantic Highlands National Bank, and the Borough of Highlands. The Monmouth County Hall of Records' large deed books for 1936, 1937, and 1938 reveal page after page of hundreds of properties taken. After Sunday, October 30, 1938, and H.G. Wells's radio drama *War of the Worlds*, people hard hit in Highlands could only wonder why the Martians would want to come to New Jersey.

Economic relief would come soon for the 10 million Americans still jobless in 1939, but at the horrific price of World War II. During the summer of 1941, Highlanders and large numbers of seasonal visitors were enjoying themselves in various social activities. Two movies were playing at the Marine Theatre at 88 Bay Avenue toward the end of July. Little did the viewers know of the import and relevance of *Sgt. York*, starring Gary Cooper and Walter Brennan, and *Caught in the Draft*, with Bob Hope and Dorothy Lamour. Within six months time, both situations would become real life—December 7, 1941, was approaching.

7. Highlands During World War II

The war was raging in Europe and more and more soldiers were stationed at Fort Hancock, so many, in fact, that Highlands began a campaign for a United Service Organization (USO) fund to support the USO facility on Sandy Hook. Because of the soldiers and their families, business was good throughout town in all the shops and not just its many taverns. Mayor Bedle and volunteers knocked on every door in town on behalf of the welfare of the boys in camp, calling it "our patriotic duty." He and Brigadier General Philip S. Gage, the post commander who spoke of the "long term neighborly feeling" between the fort and Highlands, were at the head of the parade with over 1,200 troops and two full military bands.

To help America's support of Britain and its allies in Europe, advertisements were run in the papers asking adults and kids to buy Defense Saving Stamps and Bonds at the post office. To prepare the troops for possible hostile action abroad, if and when it became necessary, there were staged a mock combat and air raid at Sandy Hook and at Highlands and all along the shore as far as Long Branch in mid-October 1941. There was a simulated blackout, sirens wailed, and Civil Defense wardens scanned the skies for enemy aircraft and the ocean for invasion ships.

After the emotional shock on Sunday, December 7, 1941, the day that has indeed lived in infamy, the burlesque air raids and military maneuvers frightened few people in Highlands, except those mothers of boys already in the army and navy and those mothers whose boys were talking of joining "to fix the Japs." Highlanders were rather philosophical about the threats of attack. Yet many parents were worried, especially as the little ones in school were drilled in air raid procedures, and came home for lunch just a bit uneasy.

People about town called each other and spoke across their fences about poor councilman George W. Hardy, how worried his wife must be about their boy Leonard, who was stationed with the U.S. Mosquito Fleet at Pearl Harbor. No word from or about him had been received so far. Yet George appeared so calm as he went about town seeking volunteers to serve just two hours a month as Air Raid Sky Watchers.

They went about their normal days' business, as best they could. Some spoke of something going on up on the hill with the Hartshornes, that the army had told the Trasks to be ready to move out of their home soon. Fort Hancock would effectively expand into the Highlands hill site (now Hartshorne Woods Monmouth County Park), developing it

Fred P. Bedle, seen here in front of his famed drugstore in 1952, served as mayor for three terms, 1933–1934, 1941–1942, and 1943–1944.

with barracks and administrative buildings to staff the Coast Artillery batteries: two 16-inch guns in Battery Lewis (still extant today) and two 6-inch gun batteries located several hundred yards away. Many of the Highlands men worked long hours in the construction of the batteries and the surrounding buildings. Some people wondered if the army would tell them too to move out of Parkertown or maybe even Water Witch, if things got bad. Could they do that? People were worried. Mayor Bedle reassured them that everything would be alright, telling them not to give in to excessive worry for that would play right into "the hands of Hitler and the Japs." Still they left Bedle's Drug shop at Bay and Miller concerned, especially the mothers and grandmothers of young draft-age men.

Mayor Bedle and the council appointed a Defense Council, charged with covering Borough Hall 24 hours a day and educating the townspeople about what they were to do in an air raid. The warning would be one long blast and three short blasts on the fire horn alarm, repeated several times. The day before Christmas, the Defense Council held a mass meeting in the school auditorium for everyone in town, so that the council could inform and educate them about air raids and civil defense.

In January 1942, Mayor Bedle's troubles from the Republican majority on the council were insignificant to the troubles the nation faced in the war. Patriotism prevailed in many aspects of life, even politics, and reduced tensions and encouraged cooperation in borough administration. The Highlands *Star* of January 22, 1942, carried a large cartoon, "Don't Be an Axis Partner," like the Rumor Monger, the Hoarder, the Duty Dodger, and the Whiner.

By February 19 that year, simulated blackouts became the real thing. Jersey Central Power and Light Company held a full blackout from 9:30 to 9:45. That made many folks uneasy, despite the prior announcements and their preparations with blackout shades (29¢ each at Siegfried's Hardware), when they looked out from the hills and saw that New York City had disappeared.

In March, two happenings brought the reality and seriousness of the war home to Highlands. On March 12 and 19, the first draft numbers were chosen by the Draft Board in Atlantic Highlands. Among the 24 names of Highlands boys were Albert Daust, Ronald Meehan, Mahlon Burdge, George Foster, Frederick Dempsey, William Black, Howard Brey, and Harry Matthews. The other event came on March 26, when the War Ration Book program was announced. All persons, men, women, children, even infants, had to register between May 4 and 7 to get a ration book of stamps, one of which was torn out at each sugar purchase. Other commodities also were controlled by rationing. Gasoline started early July 1942. Then came fuel and heating oil in November and coffee in December 1942. By the middle of January the next year, businessmen in Highlands were openly complaining how rationing was adversely affecting business, since people were not able to use their automobiles for shopping, visiting, and going out to restaurants. One big advantage of rationing was the drastically reduced highway accident and fatality count. However, even pedestrians had to abide by the stringent rules when shoes were put on rationing in February.

In March, there was a new rationing twist, the point system, whereby all processed foods, juices, fruits, vegetables, meats, soups, etc., anything in cans, jars, bottles, and even frozen foods (a relative rarity still at that time) required a certain number of ration point stamps for purchase. The whole rationing system was a complicated annoyance for most Highlanders, necessary, of course, but a nuisance still. The *Star* had a weekly column called "Ration Hints" to help readers keep pace with the changing regulations.

People who knew the right people could always buy rationed products on the black market, of course, at a premium price. The New York area even once was flooded with counterfeit ration books, sold also on the black market. Next butter was added and then all red meats in late March 1943. Things got so bad for the restaurant business in August 1944 that Tom Ross, owner of the Cedar Inn on Navesink Avenue, became fed up with the struggle and closed the place, citing shortages, rationing, and price ceilings caused by the War Department that made earning a living almost impossible. He complained, for example, that a bushel of clams used to cost $1.25 in 1941 but ran him $4.50 in August 1944, but regulations prevented him from raising his menu prices to cover the cost. The government regulators were out in force watching out for price violators and they fined Emil Aufieri in March 1945. He paid a $100 fine for overcharging on a straight whiskey and a Manhattan.

The world of the Highlanders had drastically changed and not for the better. Still the people in town tried their best to enjoy themselves to spite Hitler's Nazis and the Japanese menace. But they seemed to lose more and more of the things they were accustomed to, like the Sandy Hook boats of the Central Railroad, which would not run again even after the war since the boats themselves had been taken over by the War Department for troop carrier purposes. In July, the Coast Guard did a census and registered all boats 35 feet or longer, in case they were needed sometime, as had happened in Dunkirk. People held on to their baseball games and bowling leagues, as long as there were enough boys and men to play the sports. They had seven teams playing in two bowling leagues, the Forsgate Farms, the Ideal Diner, Captain Wheeler's, the Esso Juniors, the Lions Club, Highlands Esso, and Mohr's Tavern. They went to the movies at the Marine during the warm

A popular diversion from the tensions of World War II and the inconveniences on the home front was the sport of bowling. Seen here in 1937, Highlands Bowling was owned by George Brown. The site at 107 Bay Avenue is now an office building.

summer months and at the Atlantic. They let the delights on the motion picture screens carry them away and forget their cares. Yet also it was in the movies that they saw the news clips that showed the world at war, bringing home reminders of their young men and women in places they saw on the screen.

Women were reminded in advertisements in magazines, in newspapers, and on film at the movies that not just their men were in the war:

> You're in the Army! New Jersey housewives are a military strength and are serving today on America's home front. Many are in uniform in the Red Cross or the Motor Corps. Thousands are serving in their own homes making America stronger, healthier and better able to perform the new tasks which the times have placed upon us.

Still others were taking up the jobs their men usually did, thus allowing the men to assume more demanding combat-related work.

The advertising campaign for War Bonds was relentless throughout the entire war. For each of the seven bond drives, towns were assessed a quota according to their size, workforce, and relative affluence. The ads were attention grabbers. "War Bonds! I gave a man, will you give 10% of your salary for War Bonds?" asks a mother huddling her little boy and girl.

On August 6, 1942, Sandy Hook Light was extinguished to prevent submarines from being able to zero in on the shipping channels. This light had burned continuously since 1764, except during the very brief time it was out during the Revolutionary War. In late

August 1942, a huge lot of draft numbers was pulled and 165 Highlands boys knew that they would be called, some sooner than others, but all would be called. As they waited, they went on with their lives, although some decided to beat the draft and enlist, hoping to get a better or maybe safer duty.

Meanwhile advertisements ran weekly in the *Star* for the scrap drive: "Bomb Tagged for Tokyo! Slap the Japs! Hammer Hitler! With Your Scrap! Needed today for Victory: metals, rags, burlap, manila rope, paper, fats." The school kids at the local grammar school did their part by collecting 13,495 pounds of scrap paper in 1945.

Two encouraging stories about Highlands and the war ran in the paper in September. The first was about Lieutenant Ardeth Cunnane, daughter of Edna Cunnane, former borough clerk, of 20 Second Street. She had graduated Leonardo High in 1931 and graduated as a nurse from Bayonne Hospital in 1936. Then, she worked as a public health nurse until she came home to Highlands just before the start of the war. On November 15, 1941, she went over to Fort Hancock and enlisted in the Army Nursing Corps. When the story was written, she was on the staff at Provisional Hospital No. 2 in Honolulu, Hawaii. She wrote home often, never mentioning Pearl Harbor or any military details of war or wounded. She loved the flowers so abundant there and described the pretty native girls who wore flowers in their hair. Often she spoke of the beauty of Hawaii and of Highlands and how she missed the hills, home, and her friends and family.

The other story's star was Sergeant Robert Johnson from Waddell Avenue, where he kept pigeons. The army noted his pigeon-handling ability at Fort Dix and sent him to Fort Monmouth's signal corps, where carrier pigeons were still being handled and used in communications. Finally, Johnson went to Fort Bliss in Texas, where he worked his pigeons in hot, arid, and mountainous terrain. He went on to train other soldiers to handle the birds he liked so much since his school days in Highlands.

The whole town, without exaggeration, turned out on October 9, 1942, at Bay Avenue and Miller Street for the unveiling of the Highlands Honor Roll, a huge bulletin board containing the names of every Highlands man and woman in military service. There were 174 names with lots of blank space for the many more yet to be added as time went on. It was one of the most impressive scenes ever to take place in the borough. Not since the soldier memorial "Lest We Forget" by the bridge was unveiled was there such a total and somber response by Highlanders. Mayor Bedle and Councilman George Hardy both spoke in the ceremony, but no one remembered the words they said—all they heard and saw were the names of their men. The mothers whose boys were in service all got 8-by-12 inch cloth flags to hang in their front windows. It was red and white with a blue V, above which was a blue star for each son in service.

Mabel F. Parker sat in her home on Second Street cutting out a small gold star from a bit of cloth one November day in 1942. She had two boys in service, Sergeant Ward H. Parker, a radioman, and Samuel Thomas Parker, yeoman second class in the Coast Guard. The gold star was for her boy, Sam's star. He was dead. His cutter *Muskegat* was lost in the North Atlantic and never returned to its home port in Boston. He was only 21 and had joined the Coast Guard on September 22, 1939. Mabel Parker finished the sewing, hung the flag in the window, and thought aloud to her daughter, Lorraine, "Well, I am the first. Let's hope I am also the last mother to have to do this."

The whole town was buzzing about Mrs. Parker's loss, bringing the reality of the war being fought thousands of miles away right into the center of Highlands, right into the hearts of every person in town. Then their buzzing grew even louder when Lieutenant General Drum imposed nighttime beach restrictions on November 19, 1942. From sunset to sunrise, all unauthorized persons were to stay 300 feet clear of the ocean, bay, and river water. Boats could only be docked at registered docking places at night and should stay off the water completely if possible. Persons living in houses on the water could exit only from the land side. No cameras, telescopes, flashlights, binoculars, or signal devices were to be used in the 300-foot forbidden area. Violators were subject to prosecution or might be shot.

Good news, finally something to smile and cheer about, circulated around town. The paper said it best, "Highlands Man Hero in 'Canal'—Gallant Service against Japs," referring to Albert DePasquale. His mother reread the last letter she had from him and passed it around for others to read, for it was encouraging. "Hello, Ma, I couldn't come home for Easter. I am going on a long trip and won't see you for a long time. But keep your chin up, as God is with us, and don't worry about me. I will be okay. We must beat the Japs!" His mother followed the advice in the papers, and that spring, she started her Victory Garden in her backyard, as many others had done, knowing it was her weapon of war and could help her boy in the conflict.

Women were working in the shipbuilding yards right along side the men, there and in similar situations across the nation that summer of 1943. Each was a "Rosie the Riveter" and there were 17 million of them doing various strenuous jobs vital to the war effort. Other women took over as drivers of Army trucks, jeeps, and automobiles, anything up to

During World War II, the town of Highlands, with a total population of 2,100, sent 259 men and 5 women into service. Most of these names were recorded on the Honor Roll. (Courtesy Steve Layton.)

2.5 tons, at Fort Hancock in October that same year. Right in Highlands itself, Mrs. Louella Parker Opfermann had concealed her philanthropy for the local Episcopal church and needy families in town for years, but now many knew of her purchase of four sewing machines to allow Highlands women to make bandages for severely wounded soldiers. Across the nation, women were proving to themselves that the "weaker sex" need not be confined to the household, the hospital, or the schoolroom. They were showing that they could do anything the men could. Their world had changed and they were changing the world, which would not easily revert to pre-war thinking once the conflict was over.

In early August, posters went up in Highlands and flyers were on the counters in all the shops from the public relations officer at Fort Hancock announcing that between August 28 and August 31, the really big coastal artillery guns (the 12-inch cannons at batteries Kingman and Mills) would be test fired. Residents were advised to open all windows in the house and car, to take down pictures from the walls, and carefully wrap valuable china. There was a second period of tests on December 29 through January 1. Years later, Betty Parker Card of 254 Navesink Avenue spoke of the summer gun blasts, describing how the humid air of summer intensified the shocks felt. She remembered the first blasts were surprisingly strong but did no damage. There was a perhaps a ten-minute delay and then she felt a terrific shock and heard simultaneously a deafening blast seconds after seeing the fire from the gun across the water. At lunch, she noticed in her dining room's south wall a crack 5 feet long, jagged and wide.

That summer the army held special training maneuvers over in Water Witch on the hill, the Red Hill, off Linden Avenue and overlooking Conners hotel and bungalows. The hillside was sparsely developed compared to today, and they used it to practice running jeeps and winching gun trailers and equipment up and down the slopes.

Yet another telephoned Western Union telegram arrived for Second Street, and Chief Monahan brought this one too, for he felt it was his duty. It was for Mrs. Anna Patterson at number 52. Monahan repeated the words he heard that April 1943: Michael O. "Oats" Patterson is missing in action. At least there was hope. Then, Chief Monahan was again at the door with his hat in his hand, having taken a phoned telegram addressed to Anna Patterson. Michael's sister Mary Ann was there to bolster her mother. They heard the standard words from the adjutant general, the standard words of regret. Corporal Michael O. Patterson had been killed in action against the enemy at Kesserine Pass, Tunisia, North Africa, on March 28, 1943, in service to his country. Louis Papa, a boy from Atlantic Highlands, a friend of Oats, wrote a letter to the family. He told Mrs. Patterson how sad he was to have to tell her that he saw her son, Michael, dead after the battle, that his friend Oats did his duty, that they would be proud of him, that he often spoke of how much he missed the wonderful and beautiful waters and hills of Highlands and especially his mother and sister and friends back home in town. Months later, the family would have to relive all this grief again when Patterson's remains would arrive under military escort at the station in Atlantic Highlands, where Posten's Funeral Home would receive them. Patterson was 32 years old.

Letters of men in service were carefully censored and references to battles, equipment, and locations were blacked out, as were severe negative comments or gory descriptions, anything the censors considered not in the best interest of the war effort. To save shipping

Corporal Michael O. Patterson poses for this picture during basic training at Fort Knox in Kentucky. He was killed in action at Kesserine Pass in Tunisia on March 23, 1943. Patterson was one of 13 Highlands boys killed in World War II. (Courtesy George Patterson.)

weight and insure security, they photographed all letters. Here is an excerpt from one of the many letters Michael Patterson wrote to his sister. Dated August 1, 1942, it serves as an example of V-Mail or Victory Mail:

> Received your letter of July 21st and sure was glad to hear that you are all well and happy. Well, kid, I am the same, in the pink of condition, getting plenty of sleep . . . but it will never take the place of the states no matter what part. It can never be as beautiful as Highlands. I have talked with a number of people assigned here. They have done a lot of traveling. When I tell them about the famous lights on the hill, they always recall them and then they say that it is God's country there, and God bless them, it really is. I have sent out a number of post cards in the line of . . . around Ireland, also some comics. There is one thing that I do miss and that is the person that has given me so much comfort in life and happiness and that is my own true loving wife, Beatrice, the person that I worship . . . of ground she treads upon. I love that gal. Well, Sis, there isn't any news to say but I sure could have got in trouble over that picture of me in the paper [the *Highlands Star* of June 11, 1942]. You know southern Ireland is a hostile country and we didn't dare go near that part of the country. Well I better close now. Keep smiling and chins up. . . . Give my love to all at home and our friends. So I say so long and pleasant dreams. Will write long letter later. Your brother, Michael.

While the war brought plenty of worry, anxiety, and hardship to families in Highlands, one thing good to come out of it was the upturn in the economy. Although rationing caused scarcity of most products, prices were fixed and could not legally be exceeded. Workers in industry enjoyed a 82% pay boost over 1939, despite the cost of living being up some 27%. For sure, not everyone in Highlands benefited from the war prosperity, but enough did to be able to allow Highlands to make its quota of $35,000 for the war bond drive set in October 1943, and in November that year, Highlands raised its quota of $1,200 in the national war bond drive under the leadership of E.A. Rodriguez, adjutant of the American Legion Twin Lights Post.

Some good news arrived in town in May with the spring flowers and warmer days. Red meat had been taken off the rationing. That wasn't much of a benefit, for steaks and roasts were almost impossible to find. The Dempsey family at 24 Portland Road had some good cheer as they read in a V-mail letter from both Lieutenant Gerard and Sergeant Charles that the two boys were able to meet in England and enjoy some time together.

The summer of 1944 was a very hot and dry time for year-round and summer residents alike and put an extraordinary strain on the borough's water system. Mayor Bedle appealed to everyone to go easy on the water, using only what was really necessary. The water plant on Miller Street was pumping 540,000 gallons daily and just barely was keeping up with demand. The standpipe on the hill was empty. Mayor and council struck an emergency pact with Atlantic Highlands, and the neighboring water system was to fill the standpipe each night. However, disaster hit on August 3 before the connections could be made. A valve in the pumping station broke in the closed position at 2 a.m. and it was not repaired until well past 3 p.m. During the interval, the Highlands fire department laid

Highlands was more affected during World War II than most other towns its size due to its proximity to Fort Hancock. The railroad ran through the town continuously moving supplies, munitions, and troops as shown in this photograph taken from the bridge late in the war.

down 1,500 feet of hose between Ocean Boulevard in Atlantic Highlands and the nearest hydrant at Navesink and Linden Avenues to feed some water at least to lower Highlands. When the valve was repaired, they left the hose in place as a precaution. The police were patrolling in car and on foot watching for water use violators.

When Monahan walked up Fourth Street, all supposed he was on water patrol. However, he went straight up to Mrs. Harriet Robertson's house. She was his mother-in-law. He had already called his wife, Josephine, and asked her to come over to her mother's residence, for he had some bad news about one of the three boys in service. Sisters Marie, Alvina, and Luella were there to lend support as Mrs. Robertson opened the telegram, read it, then clutched it to her heart, and said just three words, "My boy Willard." He had been killed in a tank in one of the first assaults on the beaches at Normandy on June 6, 1944. He was 29 years old, had gone to high school in Atlantic Highlands, worked with the CCC, and had served and trained with the Red Bank National Guard units for three years. Willard's brothers, Kermit and Thomas, were in service somewhere in Europe. Years later, almost half a century later, Willard's dog tag (and five others) would be found by a French boy prospecting on the beach and eventually returned to a family member in a brief touching ceremony in Borough Hall.

During this time, Highlands was attacked not by the Germans, but by the fury of Mother Nature. The storm of the century shook Highlands to its core, when the hurricane of September 14, 1944, hit the town at 5 p.m. in the afternoon. The floodwaters rose very fast, with unexpected speed, and topped off at 4 feet deep on most of Bay Avenue and almost 5 feet near Atlantic Street. Mayor Bedle's drug shop was nearly a total wreck after its windows crashed in from the force of the water and the howling wind. Houses literally floated off their concrete foundations, both summer homes and year-round Highlanders' homes as well. Roy Guenther's bungalow on Marine Place came to rest just a few feet from Bay Avenue. Fifty residents lost everything, as their houses just crumbled and crashed around them. Still many thanked God that no one was killed or even hurt seriously. Thanks to the Civil Defense plans and drills of the early years of the war, just about everyone knew what to do. Wardens assisted the police, firemen, and first aid squads. Countless others volunteered their boats and rowed through town throwing ropes to stranded people and even swimming over to the older folks stranded on chairs on porches. All the piers, docks, and bulkheads were torn away and the amount of debris floating throughout the town was overwhelming.

Mayor Bedle and all the councilmen visited people who had taken refuge in the Grammar School, cheering them, reminding them that Highlanders always return and that they would help everyone come back to their homes as soon as possible, that these were bad times for the town but that they had seen worse in Europe in the newsreels in the movies. They told people a heartwarming story they had heard, how Archie Mount, 70 years old, a semi-invalid and a bit hard of hearing, went to sleep in his home over on Miller Street early in the storm. He figured he had been through worse. As he slept, the storm worsened until his little dog jumped up on his bed and pulled the bed clothes off him until he awakened. As he got out of bed, he found himself standing in about 3 feet of water and his hero little dog was standing on a table barking for help. An army truck took Archie Mount and his clever dog aboard the truck and kept them safe.

Mayor Bedle surveyed the devastation throughout his little town and did some estimating of the damage. He totaled a $250,000 public loss and $750,000 in private damage. How could people take it all, he wondered privately. They lose their sons and husbands to the service, some lose them permanently and forever, and now everyone he knew in lower Highlands lost much to the storm. The Highlanders were tough, neighbors helped each other, they cleaned up the mess, and they got back to work.

The town was still struggling to clean up and repair after the storm and before the winter cold set in late October when Mr. and Mrs. William Schadt of 17 Washington Avenue received some very good news about their boy, Technical Sergeant Ray M. Schadt. He had been awarded the Silver Star for heroic conduct in combat. The letter they received explained the details of his valor in battle and stated that he had been wounded during the combat in France but that he was recovering well in a hospital in England. It ended by thanking his mother on behalf of the War Department for contributing her son to the service of his country.

That November brought the elections and a degree of relief for Mayor Fred Bedle, who would not have to shoulder the responsibilities of the town for another two years. He lost the election to Meade Robertson 702 to 380 as Republicans swept the county.

On January 1, 1945, the mayor and council were sworn into office and they, like all people in Highlands, hoped the new year would be more auspicious than the last four years of war and tragedy had been. People in town and all over the nation knew the end of the war was close. Even the newsreel official Army propaganda at the movies showed a thoroughly weakened German resistance. They had failed in the Battle of the Bulge, and it was only a matter of time and more hard fighting until the Allies would enter Berlin. The newspapers carried frequent articles speculating on how things would be after the war, what would have to be done to get back onto a peace-time economy, what educational programs the returning G.I.s would have, etc.

The *Star* ran a heart-warming story, "Highlands Girl Finds Brother Her Patient in Hospital." The girl was Lieutenant Gertrude Van Kirk of Prospect Street, a nurse working in a hospital in Belgium where many of the casualties of the Battle of the Bulge were being treated. As she was making her rounds after some new patients were brought in, she heard someone yell out, "Hey, sis!" Usually her reply was "Don't sis me!" but this time she recognized the voice and bolted across a bed to be at her brother John's side. He was well enough to tell her how his squad had been advancing against the enemy when he got hit and dove into a foxhole. He lay there quite a while and two of his buddies tried to rescue him. One got killed and the other wounded in the attempt and both fell into the same foxhole. Here, they lay for 10 days until the Germans withdrew and medics could come to their aid. Van Kirk suffered severe frostbite to both feet and hands, resulting in the loss of some toes.

When the seventh war bond drive commenced in May 1945, it was clear that Highlands was not going to even come close to making its $30,000 quota. Some people felt the war was almost over and questioned the need of buying more bonds; many others just honestly could not afford it any longer, feeling they had sacrificed enough already and finding it hard to pay for the loss of all their possessions during the big storm. They had no insurance. Now they were paying rent because they could not live in their

Chief Howard Monahan (far right) poses with the members of the Highlands Police Department in 1946.

wrecked homes. Despite patriotic conscience twinges, they bought all the bonds they could afford.

The finances of the town were not much better off, either, despite a $100,000 long-term savings from renegotiating the municipal bonds at a lower interest rate. People had stopped paying their taxes and Mayor Robertson and council had no choice but to resort to tax lien sales and sales of Borough-owned properties taken in default. In February, they had 129 properties up for sale, and in May, 95 other properties were on the block. Perhaps half of all these had houses on the lots to be sold. To aggravate the financial situation yet more, the 1945 budget called for a tax rate of $63.55 per $1,000 of assessed valuation in order to pay for repairs to the water plant and damage from the big storm.

Chief Monahan's war-time humanitarian duties brought him with messages to other homes in town besides those detailed. He came about George K. "Red" Hauber, Malcolm Miller, John F. Ryan Jr., LeRoy Smith, Ernest Arnath, Kenneth Furey, and John M. Greene. He carried telegrammed messages of sadness to homes for Robert S. Matthews, Lewis Mount, Edward Minor, and Charles Rugg. Monahan had personally done this duty for relatives of 13 Highlands boys who had given their lives in service to their country.

The church bells in town rang loud and joyously for such a long time, as did the fire and first aid alarms, and car and truck horns all over in upper and lower Highlands, in

In this 1947 photograph, soldiers recently returned from World War II march along Bay Avenue on Memorial Day, May 30.

Parkertown, and in Water Witch. It was V-E Day—Victory in Europe had been declared on May 8, 1945. But for America, there was to be yet more blood, sweat, and tears in the Pacific until the time the papers carried the news of the new, terrible yet justified weapon they called the atomic bomb, dropped on Hiroshima on August 6, and another on Nagasaki before V-J Day—Victory over Japan on August 14, 1945. Again the bells, whistles, horns, and sirens pealed, wailed, and cried out in sorrow for the war's miseries and in joy for the war's end. The doors of OLPH, St. Andrew's, and the Methodist church were thrown open for overwhelmingly huge crowds of the faithful. The Reverend John M. Long of the Methodist church led a service of praise and thanksgiving with a memorial and dedication in song and words of scripture. In his message to the congregation, he urged, in view of the sacrifices of those who struggled, were wounded, and gave their lives, that they dedicate their lives, each and everyone, to making a lasting peace through the medium of the church of Christ and under the authorship of the Prince of Peace.

Lavinia Minton, of 70 Fifth Street, was there in church in her usual place with her daughter Deborah Bogue. She thanked God for the men and women who suffered so much and for the end of the terrible war. She thanked God that she was permitted to be alive to witness the glorious victory and peace. She had prayed for soldiers in four major conflicts: the Civil War, the Spanish-American War, the Great World War, and now the Second World War. She had been born Lavinia Mount in 1844, and on November 22, she would be 101 years old!

8. After the War to the Present

As the G.I.s returned home to Highlands and started families, there was a major housing shortage. The Highlands men would have none of the tract houses being built in places like River Plaza; they returned to Highlands, their home where there began a large-scale conversion of summer bungalows into year-round homes all over town. The conversion move was accelerated by the diminishing desirability of Highlands for summer vacationers throughout the late 1950s and 1960s, making more and more summer places available for year-round use either on the original sites or moved and expanded on other sites.

Soon after the last Central Railroad of New Jersey train left Highlands on November 30, 1958, and the line was abandoned from Highlands to Atlantic Highlands, the 60-foot-wide right-of-way became available to become a borough street named Shore Drive. The old Water Witch station and other accessory buildings were demolished and the land from the Atlantic Highlands border to Water Witch Avenue awaited development. As early as 1953, it had been suggested that the line running from the bridge to the Water Witch station be given up for use as a borough street. Once a new roadway was in place, the land from Water Witch to Miller Street and slightly beyond also was available for eventual building.

The need for housing following World War II was hardest on the many less affluent Highlands families (78 houses had been identified as sub-standard) unable to meet the high cost of purchase, conversion, and/or rental. The first municipal Housing Authority looked to the U.S. government for affordable housing assistance and found it in the government funding of 30 apartments of Jennie Parker Manor in 1953–1954. The three apartment complexes, locally called "the project," were constructed on the site of the defunct Highlands incinerator, on Navesink Avenue between Water Witch Avenue and Rogers Street.

The post-war housing shortage in Highlands and some other bayshore communities was met by the creation of so-called mobile home parks. Two found acceptance in Highlands on the western section of town. Paradise Mobile Home Park, with some 18 units, located at the end of Locust Street along the border with Atlantic Highlands, was owned and operated by Burtis Perry since 1951 (sold to John Torok in June 1953). The establishment of Shadow Lawn Trailer Park below Mt. Mitchill on Route 36 and Ocean Boulevard in 1952 prompted the Borough to draft ordinances regulating such housing.

Lloyd Cottrell, who as child was part of the initial discovery of gold in Highlands, is pictured c. 1966 with his son, Rob, on their dock in Highlands.

Shadow Lawn originally was exclusively an adults-only establishment with its units arranged around its own pool and gardens.

More land was created in 1964 as the result of river channel dredging. This time, Conners was the primary beneficiary, as it received some 200 feet of sand in front of the hotel, enabling the Black brothers to open in 1965 the locally important Conners Pool Club with a large parking area to accommodate guests' cars.

The most exciting thing to happen for people in Highlands after the V-E Day and V-J Day celebrations marking the end of the war was the Highlands Gold Rush of 1948. People in the town often used to speak of pirate gold and buried treasure just waiting to be found some day. There were intriguing stories of years ago such as the *Water Witch* novel of James Fenimore Cooper, which told of pirates, smuggling, and mystery, and "The Legend of Cudjo," a short story in which the black pirate Cudjo met a horrible death while guarding his captain's treasure. Highlanders became convinced of the truth of legends told of Captain Kidd burying treasure somewhere about town.

However, the hardworking fishermen in the Highlands had little time to spend in such alluring notions and dreams of getting rich quick. People like the Parkers, the Maxsons, and Cottrells had always worked hard and struggled to make a living from the river, bay, and ocean waters around Highlands.

On Wednesday, April 7, 1948, two fishermen were returning home after a very wearing ordeal at sea. Old William R. Cottrell stepped into the inch or so of water along the beach and noticed something by his foot. He bent down, picked it up, and showed it to his boy, Lloyd. It was a gold coin about the size of a 50¢ piece. Then later with relatives and some trusted friends, they returned to find another, then another in the watery sands at the foot of Cedar Street, there in Highlands.

The next day, no Cottrells went to sea. They found an excuse to stay on the beach, and after the others had gone off in their boats, they picked up more gold treasure coins, a total of six in all, they claimed. Satisfied there were no more, they began to share the news of their good fortune with friends around town. The word spread fast. There was no stopping it until everyone had heard it and someone called the newspapers. That Friday, even the *New York Times* ran the story on its front page. The *Daily News*, the *Newark Evening News*, the *Press*, and later the local weeklies such as the *Register* and the Highlands *Star* covered the excitement with stories and pictures.

Because of the publicity, the next day the town of Highlands went wild, with locals and out-of-town tourists alike, as they swarmed over the sands of the beach at Cedar Avenue in search of gold. They called themselves prospectors like the ones in the Alaska Klondike of 1896. The newspapers called them "48ers," reminiscent of the great California gold strike and its 49ers nearly a century before. Many of the Highlanders called them "damned fools" for behaving the way they did. They arrived in large numbers: 300, then 500, then 5,000 in all, coming to town by car, truck, train, rowboat, and foot. They came to town thinking and saying "Goin' to the Highlands, find gold, and retire."

Shopkeepers saw a profit to be made, putting up signs that read "Gold Field This Way," "Gold Digging Tools for Sale," and "Shovels for Rent." They sold out every shovel, hoe, rake, bucket, pail, and sifter they had. The variety stores, hardware shops, diners, and even Bahrs Restaurant along Bay Avenue were fast cleaned out, and even the 15 taverns in town at that time struggled to keep up with the demand.

Gold rush fever drove these young men and hundreds of others from as far away as New York to dig and sift tons of river beach sand off Cedar Avenue in search of elusive buried treasure in April 1948. In all, perhaps two dozen eighteenth-century Portuguese gold coins were found.

Exactly how many gold coins were found is not certain as press accounts tell of 21, 28, or 30. Perhaps the true number was kept secret in fear of thieves or state and local government authorities. The gold value alone was worth $18 and lucky diggers were offered $20, $50, and $200 each by shrewd or naive collectors. Today each would bring about $2,500 from a dealer. The coins were all Portuguese and bore the portrait of King John V with dates such as 1748, during his reign, and inscriptions in Latin. They were treasure items, indeed, but not from old Captain Kidd, who died on a London gallows in 1701. Nor were they from a British ship known to have wrecked in the river at Highlands in 1744.

The most likely explanation of their origin is that the British military, in their tactical retreat to New York via Sandy Hook, then an island, after their defeat at the Battle of Monmouth in June 1778, somehow accidentally dropped overboard in their haste and lost in the swift river channel a bag of coins (the Portuguese coins, by the way, were of high purity gold and were accepted by other governments as legal tender) used to pay troops or secure supplies. In modern times, the channel was dredged some years before the gold rush and the sand was pumped up to widen the beaches in the Highlands.

At this writing on the Highlands Gold Rush, 50 years later, there are still some prospectors in town who may tell their grandchildren how they looked for gold on the beach, how money flowed like the floodwaters in town, and how so many people went crazy for a time in the Highlands long ago.

Another form of gold fever returned to Highlands two years later when the town joyously celebrated its 50th anniversary Golden Jubilee. Mayor Joseph A. Dempsey was the honorary chairman of the Jubilee Committee assisted by 53 member-workers headed by President Arthur Joseph. The workers on the very large, gold-covered journal beautifully printed in precise off-set, which contained the very first history of the Borough ever done and written by nationally known author Fletcher Pratt, were John Flemm, Benjamin Gruber, Viola Horan, and Fletcher Pratt.

The program of events in August 1950 were a fireworks display on Plum Island on August 18; a baby parade and coronation of the queen on August 19; a block dance on Bay Avenue evening on August 19; a grand parade and dedication of the Living War Memorial at Kavookjian Field on August 20; a children's program at HES on August 21; a donkey baseball game on August 22; Scout Day on August 23; a game night at the yacht club and firehouse on August 23; swimming races in yacht basin and a talent show in HES on August 24; a baseball game and a patriotic night at the American Legion Hall on August 25; a dedication of the First Aid Building, a firemen's demonstration, and the Golden Jubilee banquet on August 26.

The people of Highlands, both residents and longtime summer vacationers, had good reason to be happy about and proud of their little town and the celebration of its Golden Jubilee and 50 years of progress. Certainly Highlands was as well off as most towns in the county and, in the minds of Highlanders, probably better off than most places along the Raritan Bay shore. Back in 1947, they opened the Water Witch Boat Basin, smaller than, but as attractive as, the municipal yacht harbor over in Atlantic Highlands. Furthermore, nearly every spot on the river in town had party boats, boat rentals, and small private marinas to attract summer shore vacationers. They read with excitement, pleasure, and

The Highlands boat basin is seen here from Washington Street looking across to the yacht club headquarters c. 1955.

some annoyance about their town and themselves in the novel *The Swamp Willow*, written by summer Highlander Edwina Elroy and released by a major national publisher, G.P. Putnam's Sons, in 1947.

These were the good times—the Highlands days in the youth of so many middle-aged and older people who moved away, yet kept alive in their minds and hearts a sea of memories about summers spent on Gravelly Point, in Conners Bungalows, by Roxy's, at Honey Suckle Lodge, Rhodart's on Fifth Street, and Neimark's.

These idyllic days in the borough, however, started to show some signs of decline caused by forces and events largely beyond the ability of anyone in town to realize, to prevent, or to control. For example, in 1950, the Central Railroad removed its bridge at Highlands and replaced its station with a meager shelter, having in 1948 abandoned its line from Highlands to Long Branch as unprofitable. In August 1951, two omens of trouble in the near future were, first, the railroad's plan to curtail or eliminate all service from Highlands to Matawan, and second, the route of the proposed Garden State Parkway was settled, effectively and completely bypassing lucrative auto traffic from Highlands and the rest of the bayshore. The result of these two would prove catastrophic for Highlands and its business.

Throughout the duration of the war, feelings of patriotic unity tended to keep political party differences and disagreements in check and under control. However, in the four years since the war's end, subtle political maneuverings began to erode the old standards of town politics until on February 10, 1949, Republicans, Democrats, the Taxpayers Association, and the Business Organization, 458 registered voters in all, started a petition for a governmental change. They wanted a non-partisan, three-person commission form of rule, citing partisan squabbling as counterproductive for Highlands' best interests, with distant political bosses controlling council voting from behind the scenes. It was defeated, but not soundly so, 590 to 535 on March 29, 1949.

Bitter partisan attacks took place in council sessions, reminiscent of the McCarthyism rampant in the U.S. Congress, during the terms of Mayors Joseph Dempsey and William Fehlhaber, resulting in Fehlhaber's resignation rather than being subjected to and forced to participate in the venomous political diatribes at council sessions. Animosity intensified by the year's financial plight and crisis the borough was caught in. The tax rate for 1951 jumped $32.66 over 1950 to $118 per $1,000 assessed value, necessitated by gross overspending and a rise in uncollected taxes. The Taxpayers Association assaulted the council, and Democrats and Republicans assaulted each other, screaming over a borough budget of $243,451 and a school budget at $63,708. Again, an attempt was made to eliminate political wrangling from borough government, and on October 24, 1952, the council decided to put a non-binding referendum question on the November ballot, "Shall Highlands abandon its present form of government and adopt one of the forms of the Faulkner Committee for small municipalities." This like the last one was defeated.

In March 1955, the issue of the railroad forsaking Highlands came up again, pitting councilmen against each other and businessmen and commuters against developers hoping to have a new street (Shore Drive) to build houses along. Protesters yelled that without the trains, the town would soon become a ghost town and would result in a serious detriment for residents and businesses. On Friday, January 13, 1956, the bitter raging on the council continued between Councilmen Guiney and Newton and Hartsgrove. Guiney questioned the ethics of his fellow councilmen concerning the hiring and firing of borough employees. Hartsgrove offered a resolution to hire his brother, Wallace Hartsgrove, to fill a vacancy created by his firing an employee in the borough streets department. A majority voted with Hartsgrove, resulting in the streets department consisting of Councilman Herbert Hartsgrove as chairman and Wallace Hartsgrove and William Hartsgrove, all three of whom were brothers. On January 27, 1956, the council meeting was again chaotic when Councilman Hartsgrove lashed out at the press for using the hiring of his brother as a political football and Councilman Newton charged the press with having a field day with Borough of Highlands issues. Hartsgrove said that he had been a member of the Highlands governing body 15 years and that this was the first time that he had hired a relative. He explained that his brother, Wallace, was unemployed and had 11 children to feed. "If it was your brother, any of you would of done the same." Both Newton and Hartsgrove resigned their posts with less than a month left in their terms.

Finally, fed up with political bitterness hindering true progress for the people of Highlands, voters achieved a change in form of borough government, to be effective July 1, 1956, when the borough's first non-partisan council was installed. This change came about through a referendum that had been held in November 1955, in which registered voters of the borough approved the change 635 to 404, with a view to end the interminable political rivalry and bickering plaguing the borough for many years. According to the Faulkner Act Plan B—non-partisan—of small borough government on May 8, 1956, 5 candidates were elected from a field of 12; they were Herman J. Black (773), James H. McGough (741), Alexander F. Bahrs (709), Robert G. Diebold (684), and Cornelius Guiney Jr. (684). Under this system, it was up to the council to elect one of the council members to serve as mayor.

When they elected Cornelius "Neil" Guiney Jr. to serve as mayor, Guiney began an unprecedented period of leadership in the Borough of Highlands, lasting a total of 20 years of relative political peace and progress in two ten-year stretches, running July 1, 1956, through June 30, 1965, and July 1, 1974, through December 31, 1983. It was a remarkable achievement.

During the first Guiney years, some significant events took place to benefit Highlands. Foremost, political bickering and obstruction practically came to a halt on council, followed by dedication of the present Borough Hall, Police Station, and Fire Department on October 8, 1961. Also, the Twin Lights were taken out of Borough control by the New Jersey Bureau of Parks in 1962 and were named a National Historic Site. The Henry Hudson Regional School opened in September 1962 for Highlands and Atlantic Highlands students in grades 7 through 12 studying together, and OLPH's new school building opened in September 1963 for grades kindergarten through 8.

Other events, however, were not so favorable for the town. Sandy Hook State Park opened on July 14, 1962, with massive traffic jams along Route 36 from Highlands to Leonardo and the CRRNJ train cars left Highlands on November 30, 1958, for the last time. The park literally siphoned off from Highlands legions of summer tourists descending in record numbers from northern New Jersey in their automobiles. The loss of the trains was more symbolic of the decline from the great days of summer tourism prior to 1950 than real, although it did effectively isolate Highlands from city employment opportunities for residents. These coupled with the massive devastation of two major storms and floods, first from Hurricane Donna on September 12, 1960, and then from the northeast storm on March 6, 1962, brought the town to an unprecedented low.

The effects of the powerful March 6, 1962 storm were devastating for Highlands, with floodwaters more than 3 feet deep in front of well-known Parrot Delicatessen on Water Witch Avenue, opposite Huddy Park. (Courtesy Lola Adolf.)

James T. White demonstrates in this image the use of the hoe in harvesting clams. White served as mayor from 1968 to 1974 and again in 1989. In 1995, the local clam depuration plant was named in his honor for years as a civil servant, dedicated schoolteacher, and clammer advocate.

Two of the three borough public beaches, the Miller Street beach and parking lot and the South Bay Avenue beach just south of the present bridge, were purchased on April 1, 1926, for $10,000 and $5,200, respectively. The third beach at the Community Center was added in June 1978.

In June 1978, the Borough built its second Community Center structure, with tennis courts, beach, and parking lot near the intersection of Beach Boulevard and Central Avenue on the last section of the land created by the river dredging of the 1930s. Highlands had an active Senior Citizen organization since 1965 (re-organized in 1972) and an ever-growing number of older residents hard-pressed to meet housing costs of taxes, maintenance, and rents. Park Towers Senior Residence, providing 94 one-bedroom apartments in a five-story building, was erected at 215 Shore Drive and dedicated on June 21, 1986.

In another significant development on approximately 1 acre of riverfront property, the James T. White Clam Depuration Plant was opened in July 1995, with boat dockage, a processing and storage building, and parking.

The beaches and parks in Highlands have a history going back many years. The park now called Huddy Park at Water Witch and Bay Avenues had been in existence since at least the time of World War I, when the *Register* reported summer train commuters to the city had victory gardens that they tended and picked going to and from the station at Water Witch. In about 1947, Councilman Thomas Lyons was responsible for the Borough's improvement of the park, with major landfill of the low and wet areas and landscaping by Lovett Nursery of Little Silver. It was at this time that the area was named Huddy Park with the transfer of the Huddy monument from across the street to its present location. Veterans' Park, comprised of 2.5 acres, had a troubled beginning with the council in 1983–84 and was called Waterfront Park.

The very large area of Kavookjian Field on Navesink Avenue actually is not in the Borough of Highlands at all, but lies in Middletown Township; it is, however, administered under the Borough's recreation department. This field, with its dedicatory plaques and monument, stands as a "living war memorial" for all Highlands veterans who served in time of war and was a gift to Highlands from resident and benefactor Haik Kavookjian in 1950.

The two public schools in the borough, Highlands Elementary School, built in 1931, and Henry Hudson Regional School, built in 1962, have precluded some dozen acres from residential or commercial development.

The first of many condominium projects, Twin Lights Terrace, was begun in December 1973 and when completed covered the hillside south of Hillside Avenue and the hilltop adjacent to Henry Hudson Regional with 160 units spread over 10 buildings. Next, in June 1974, the foundation of Top of the East high-rise condominium (now called Eastpointe) was laid by the Snyder-Westerlind Corp. on Mt. Mitchill's Ocean Boulevard, barely within the Borough of Highlands border near what once was the site of the famous Log Cabin Inn (destroyed by fire 1953). The completed building was opened a year later in June 1975, standing 15 stories tall with 166 units. The proposal by the company to erect a twin tower across the border, now Mt. Mitchill Overlook Park, was defeated by Atlantic Highlands authorities.

At Conners, the first row of bungalows, the eastern side, was taken down in 1978 to erect 60 condominium apartments (today's Sandpiper Condominiums), an enterprise immensely more profitable for the Black family and appropriate to the age than the

Eastpointe Condominium was originally called Top of the East when it was opened on Mount Mitchill by Snyder-Westerlind Corps.

Express 1, *a large passenger, high-speed catamaran, is seen nearing the end of its 45-minute Highlands-Manhattan run. Express Navigation, now called Seastreak, and New York Fast Ferry have several boats on this popular commuter route.*

bungalows of times past. By 1984, only one bungalow remained and still is used as the office for the 24 garden apartment rentals of Conners Village at 328 Shore Drive (site of the western row of bungalows). Very recently, almost the last of the old Conners Cedar Grove, the hotel and two houses, was torn down, along with the pool and cabana complex, to provide increased parking for commuters on the Seastreak ferry, making daily runs to New York's Pier 11 and East Thirty-Fourth Street docks. Only the Carriage House, now also apartments, remains from the "good old days" of Conners in Water Witch.

Marina on the Bay has 42 condominium units, with the old Highlands Marina still in operation and accessible from Bay Avenue, constructed in 1988 on the site older Highlanders remember as Neimark's.

Other condominiums are Highlands Shores, Hillside at Highlands, Ferry Landing Condominiums, Bayview Condominiums, East Manor Square (site of Martin House–Alpine Manor), Gateway Villas, Wyndmoor on the Highlands, Hilltop Terrace, Bay Pointe, Hilltop at Highlands, Seacrest, Gateway, Horizon at Highlands (conversion of the defunct clothing factory), and Vista Bay. Condominium construction continues at the time of this writing with some 20 units of Highlands on the Bay being erected on the old Roxy's Boats beach and parking site (later Long John's restaurant, still later Bermuda Schwartz restaurant and bar) on Beach Boulevard in Water Witch. The nearly 1,000 condominium units have added substantial tax ratables to the Borough's tax rolls without putting excessive strains on either the schools or municipal services, increasing the average selling price of Highlands homes considerably. However, they also have been blamed for all the ills of the community. Former mayor Neil Guiney Jr. often spoke in their defense, saying, "The condos could change the town around. . . . [if] the intelligent and talented owners would become involved with borough affairs."

While rentals account for some 50% of all residential units today (roughly the same as in 1900) and may be as much as 55% (if illegal rentals are included), the development of groups of apartments has been small. The first is thought to have been the six units at 47–57 Bay Avenue, the former site of the famous Highlands merry-go-round, which was leveled by fire about 1960. Conners Village apartments at 328 Shore Drive with its 24 units was constructed next. The 16 apartments, called Monmouth Highlands Apartments and located at 37 Navesink Avenue, were built on the site of the home of famous actor Neil Burgess. Recently small apartment groups have been built by local developer Roger Mumford at 65 Miller Street and at 18 Navesink Avenue on sites that were formerly zoned as commercial, thus transforming derelict and unprofitable business locations into eye-appealing residential tax ratables. At this time, only one large tract of land remains undeveloped, the space on Shrewsbury Avenue, with river access, opposite Jackson Street, where Johnny's Landing and the Jackson Hotel were located.

During Guiney's second term as mayor, from July 1, 1974, through 1983, two major changes took place which have negatively affected the government and management of the borough. First, civil service was approved for borough employees by a referendum on November 4, 1975, bringing out 60% of all registered voters and being approved of 591 to

This hand-drawn postcard from the 1930s accurately depicts William Conners's Cedar Grove Hotel and Bungalows. In 1964, the site received a new 200-foot-deep beach from the dredging spoils, allowing construction of the Conners Pool and Cabana complex in the lower right corner of this picture. The hotel and pool complex was demolished to make space for automobile parking for ferry commuters of Express Navigation (now Seastreak).

419. The regulations, prompted by the January 13, 1956 streets department affair and workers seeking job security and better working conditions, took effect with unalterable permanency on December 18, 1975. Second, a petition with more than the required 500 signatures was filed with council on August 11, 1976, to put a government change question on the November 1, 1976 ballot at which 1,803 voters (78% of 2,321 registered voters) came out to approve the change 1,031 to 591. This was the heaviest voter turnout in Highlands history. The new government was the Faulkner Act Plan C for Small Municipalities, a partisan structure with a June primary before the November election and the successful candidates taking office the following January 1. Furthermore, according to this plan, a mayor would be elected for a three-year term and four councilmen would be elected. These council members would choose by lot an initial one- or two-year term. Thereafter, the four councilmen would each have a three-year term with staggered elections being held every year in November. The Faulkner Act specified that "the new government shall take effect January 1 after the next general election," in November 1977. Thus, the new government took effect on January 1, 1978, and the old form of government was still in effect in May 1977, at which the successful candidates took office on July 1, 1977, and remained in office until January 1, 1978.

The first partisan election in Highlands in 22 years was held in November 1977 with 1,708 of the 2,500 registered voters casting ballots for a new mayor, Cornelius J. Guiney Jr. (737), and for councilmen: Ernest Vaughan (712), Vincent Mendes (710), John Rodgers (840), and Anthony Bucco (602).

Guiney, who would continue as mayor six more years, offered, with typical philosophical insight, his opinion on government forms on November 11, 1977. "It isn't going to make any difference," he said, "what form of government is in Highlands. It's the

Mayor Cornelius Guiney is pictured here in 1975 with Mrs. Clara Dempsey as they unfurl a Monmouth County banner.

The Diamond Jubilee Firemen's Parade ran the length of Bay Avenue on August 23, 1975, and included a neighboring department's 1917 Ford ladder truck.

people who hold office that make the difference. You can have the best form of government and terrible people in it and the town will be terrible. Or you can have the worst form of government and good people elected and the town will be fine." Guiney's comments were prompted specifically by borough troubles during the time of Mayor James T. White, between Guiney's two mayoral terms. On December 27, 1973, the Monmouth County grand jury censured borough councilmen Richard Gill, Robert Waters, C. Paul Case, Luke Penta, and Mayor White, along with Building Inspector Martin Fehlhaber, for gross impropriety in handling borough affairs. It indicted Penta on two counts of misconduct in office and soliciting a reward for his official vote. However, on December 12, 1974, Superior Court Judge Pat McGann cleared Penta of all wrong doing in so far as the State proofs failed to meet the standards of criminality in the state statutes.

In contrast to the adverse publicity in the local papers generated by these improprieties came Highlands' 75th anniversary, the Diamond Jubilee Celebration, with Mayor Guiney as the honorary chairman of the event, supported by the good services of Mrs. Clara Dempsey (chairperson) and Mrs. Agnes R. Nash, Mrs. Joseph Sherry, Cornelius J. Guiney III, and James W. Brydon in charge of the celebratory journal. Besides these, there were 22 committee members who worked hard to make the festivities significant and enjoyable. This was a tribute to the dedication of citizens back in 1975, something becoming almost non-existent in today's times.

The celebration was confined to the warmer months of May, June, and especially August 1975, and included many activities, such as a balloon release and distance contest from Twin Lights on May 17; a declaration ceremony in front of Borough Hall on June 2; sailboat races on June 21; an evening talent contest in the elementary school on August 7;

151

New Jersey State Assemblyman Joseph Azzolina returned to the Highlands of his youth to award prizes to bashful winners of the baby parade on August 10, 1975.

a softball game (women versus police department) and a donkey baseball game at Henry Hudson's field the morning of August 9; a baby parade with centenarian Haik Kavookjian, the originator of the first such parade, on August 10; a bicycle decorating contest and parade on August 11; a clam bake on August 13; a dedication of Gertrude Ederle Park (with the New Jersey Lottery Drawing) on August 14; a swim meet at Conners, with Miss Ederle presenting the awards, on August 15; Veterans' Alliance parade on August 16; a frisbee tournament in Kavookjian Field on August 17; a band concert by HHR band at Twin Lights on August 18; a donkey baseball game in Kavookjian Field on August 19; an evening rock concert in Huddy Park on August 20; an elementary schoolchildren's dawn patrol at Monmouth Park on August 21; Highlands Day at the Races on August 22; 75th-anniversary parade (with Clydesdale horses) on Bay Avenue on August 23; and church services of all denominations in Huddy Park on August 24.

The acrid nature of political animosity so typical of Highlands' government noted earlier was often counterbalanced by other, equally strong but benevolent forces at work in town, especially in times of physical crisis. Storms have frequently battered the Highlands shore, and homes and businesses took severe beatings causing a setback to any progress and advance achieved in previous years. Highlands, given its location, has been vulnerable to severe flooding caused by violent coastal storms. Those during the time of the borough struck with ferocity March 1–2, 1914; December 8, 1914; December 15, 1931; November 10, 1932; September 21, 1938; October 28, 1943; September 14, 1944; November 17, 1953; September 12, 1960; March 6, 1962; December 19, 1974; and March 29, 1984.

The behavior of Highlanders during the most recent severe storm's destruction and flooding, that of December 11–12, 1992, can serve as the example of Highlands' spirit typical in all previous times. Bob Hunter, proprietor of the Clam Hut Restaurant on the Shrewsbury River, lamented, "We were all almost wiped out by the nor'easter's force and we closed down for a week or so. All our decks and docks were destroyed. It was the fishermen who helped us the most. During the last six months they have replaced roofs and most of the docks and piers along the river." Clammer Richard Maxson, secretary of the Baymen's Association, explained, "Many fishermen are also carpenters. We had the highest tide ever recorded here. The December nor'easter was a terrible storm. . . . Highlands is still a fishermen's town, although there are condos and homes filled with New York commuters, with a great spirit. It is a unique area along the coast." Robert Cottrell, a fifth-generation lobsterman, agreed about the unique spirit of help and cooperation in the borough. "Fishermen have to be self-sufficient," he said. "Most of us can do anything, including repairing our boats. We lost all our docks during the storm, the worst I have ever seen. So fishermen helped to rebuild." Mayor Richard Schwartz, businessman and resident, commented, "We had four days of extremely high tides and that created a disaster for the area. All the residents were affected. But everybody in the borough pulled together. That's typical of the Highlands: People helping people in time of need."

Robert D. Wilson, mayor from 1984 to 1989, was a person who helped Highlands through its difficult times. Wilson grew up on a potato farm and was a sanitation worker before entry into the glamorous world of actors, movies, and Hollywood celebrities as a

A hardworking, sympathetic, and dedicated Highlands citizen, Robert D. Wilson served as mayor between 1984 and 1989.

propman and actor on films such as *Tootsie*, *The Exorcist*, and *Midnight Cowboy*. He never forgot his origins, despite the Hollywood glitz, preferring to discuss Highlands rather than his film work with journalists. He was very dedicated to the issues in Highlands. He saw the town coming back in a big way and making a valuable contribution to the county. He did not want to see the little man pushed out, such as having Paradise Trailer Park residents moved out to make room for condos. With some 5,000 people in Highlands, he wanted to represent the little man and the big man, thinking he could be fair to both.

He championed the firemen, first aid members, police, clammers, senior citizens, kids, and all people who volunteered in town. He saw himself as just another volunteer, although mayor, fortunately with an occupation that allowed him financial freedom to work for Highlands. Once, Wilson came in a hired ambulance to a borough council meeting, where he voted on a critical issue, relatively shortly after undergoing a multiple heart bypass operation and then returned to the hospital. On another occasion, he hired a float-plane to fly from a remote filming location to Highlands so that his vote would be counted. People said the following of Bob Wilson: "He did his best for everyone in the borough"; "A good mayor and a good friend to everyone in Highlands"; and "A fine mayor and always had the interests of the residents at heart." He was a real Santa Claus, dressed up to look like Bob Wilson, collecting money and spending much of his own to personally purchase toys and gifts for Highlands kids.

Wilson planned to retire from his profession, to live with his wife, Dotty, at 66 Miller Street and devote himself full time to helping Highlands become a finer place. However, on a movie set in Rahway State Prison for *Escape* with Sylvester Stalone, he died suddenly 5:30 p.m. on March 2, 1989, at age 62. The town recreation/community center was named in his honor, the Robert D. Wilson Memorial Community Center, as a tribute

By an act of the Borough Council on March 22, 1989, the recreation center became the Robert D. Wilson Memorial Community Center.

This scene captures Highlands from the beach on Sandy Hook c. 1910, when life moved slower along the river and in the hills, and it was simpler to find "Solid Comfort." (Courtesy Dorn's Collection.)

to his dedication to the town, its senior citizens, and its youth. This was done at a Council meeting without its mayor on March 22, 1989, the 89th birthday of the Borough of Highlands.

As this story of the life of Highlands and the Borough of Highlands comes to a close, there is perhaps no better way to conclude it than to read the centennial message of the Highlands Borough Council as follows:

> The Mayor and Council of the Borough of Highlands would like to welcome you all to a Centennial Celebration of 100 Years of Highlands history! Over the past century the Borough of Highlands has seen numerous changes, has weathered monstrous storms, has watched several wars come and go and has seen a millennium pass into history. However, through all of life's turmoil Highlands, its residents and its businesses continue to persevere and to prosper. This is a continuing testament to our town and its people.
>
> As we look back upon the past 100 years, we wonder what the founding fathers of Highlands thought as they launched a brand new town on March 22, 1900. What would they say if they could see Highlands today? We know that their priorities and problems were somewhat different from ours today. Back in those times the town looked much different from the way it does today. Houses, businesses and people have come and gone; but now others have taken their places. Yet through it all, through all those years the Borough of Highlands remains.

Looking forward, the next years seem very promising for the Borough. In the early 1990s several programs were put into place to insure that Highlands will be alive and well for the next 100 years and beyond. Borough operations have been streamlined and cost saving measures have been implemented. Through the Neighborhood Preservation Program (NPP) the town was able to improve its appearance and that of numerous residential and business properties. Additionally several grants were sought and received by the Borough to improve its infrastructure such as its roads, parks, bulkheads and a host of other things. Through the creation of the Business Improvement District (BID) our town's businesses have taken the initiative to determine their own destinies and to help improve the town at the same time. The result of all of this is a town that is ready to take on the next decade, the next century, and the next millennium.

So on this Centennial Anniversary we would like to say "Happy Birthday Highlands!" May you continue to prosper and grow well into the next century and beyond!

This scene from the early twentieth century harks back to Highlands' romantic past as a summer resort and captures its tranquil setting and memorable landscape.

BIBLIOGRAPHY

Adler, David A. *Gertrude Ederle, America's Champion Swimmer*. New York: Gulliver Books, 2000.

Applegate, John A. *A History of Monmouth County, New Jersey, 1664–1920*. 3 vols. New York: Lewis Historical Publishing Co., 1922.

Atlantic Highlands Journal. Atlantic Highlands, 1925–1970.

Barber, John, and Henry Howe. *Historical Collections of New Jersey: Past and Present*. 1844, 1865, Spartanburg, SC: The Reprint Co., 1966.

Bryant, William Cullen, ed. *Picturesque America, or, the Land We Live In*. 2 vols. New York: D. Appleton and Co., 1872.

Cooper, James Fenimore. *The Water Witch, or the Skimmer of the Seas*. New York: Ams Press, 1930.

Courier. Middletown, 1965–2001.

Cunningham, John T. "The New Jersey Shore . . . Highlands, Hook and Bay." *Newark Sunday News Magazine*. 3 March 1957.

Eid, Joseph. *Jersey Central Traction Company, Trolley to the Bayshore*. Eatontown: Joseph Eid, 1981.

Ellis, Franklin. *History of Monmouth County, New Jersey*. 1885. Cottonport, LA: Polyanthos, Inc., 1974.

Elroy, Edwina. *The Swamp Willow*. New York: G.P. Putnam's Sons, 1947.

Fryatt, F.E. "The Navesink Highlands." *Harper's New Monthly Magazine*. September 1879.

Gabrielan, Randal. *Sandy Hook*. Charleston, SC: Arcadia Publishing, 1999.

Gallo, Tom. *Henry Hudson Trail, Central R.R. of N.J.'s Seashore Branch*. Charleston, SC: Arcadia Publishing, 1999.

Heritage '76, a Bicentennial Commemoration. The *Asbury Park Press*. July 1976.

"Highlands Borough." *Monmouth Press*. 31 March 1900.

"Highlands Digs in for Plenty." *The Shore Press*. 2 December 1934.

Highlands, New Jersey, Borough Council Ordinances, Edition of 1909. Red Bank: The Standard Press, 1909.

Highlands, New Jersey, Golden Jubilee: Mountains, River, Ocean, 1900–1950. Highlands: Borough of Highlands, 1950.

Highlands, New Jersey: 1900–1975, Diamond Jubilee. Highlands: Borough of Highlands, 1975.

King, John P. *The Highlands*. Dover, NH: Arcadia Publishing, 1995.

———. *Views of Highlands, a Pleasant Land to See*. Highlands: Wolf Press, 1996.

Kobbe, Gustav. *The New Jersey Coast and Pines*. Short Hills: 1889.

Leonard, Thomas H. *From Indian Trail to Electric Rail*. Atlantic Highlands: Atlantic Highlands Journal, 1923.

Lunny, Robert M., ed. *Juet's Journal, The Voyage of the* Half Moon *from 4 April to 7 November, 1609*. Newark: New Jersey Historical Society, 1959.

McKenzie, Clyde L., Jr. *The Fisheries of Raritan Bay*. New Brunswick: Rutgers University Press, 1992.

Marconi, Degna. *My Father, Marconi*. New York: McGraw Hill, 1962.

Methot, June. *Up and Down the River*. Navesink: Whip Publishing, 1980.

———. *Up and Down the Shore*. Navesink: Whip Publishing, 1988.

Morford, H.T. *Fifty Years Ago, a Brief History of the 29th Regiment N.J. Volunteers in the Civil War*. Hightstown: Longstreet House, 1990.

Moss, George H., Jr. *Another Look at Nauvoo to the Hook*. Sea Bright: Ploughshare Press, 1990.

———. *Early Views of the Twin Lights and the Highlands of Navesink*. Sea Bright: Ploughshare Press, 1996.

———. *Steamboat to the Shore*. Sea Bright: Ploughshare Press, 1966, 1972.

Peterson, Russell. *Another View of the City*. New York: McGraw Hill, 1967.

Red Bank Register. 27 June 1878–3 July 1964.

Reussille, Leon. *Steam Vessels Built in Old Monmouth 1841–1894*. Brick Township: J.I. Farley, 1975.

Salter, Edwin, and George C. Beekman. *Old Times in Old Monmouth*. Freehold: Monmouth Democrat, 1874.

Guthorn, Peter J. *The Sea Bright Skiff and Other Jersey Shore Boars*. New Brunswick: Rutgers University Press, 1971.

"Seaside as a Borough." *Monmouth Press*. 14 April 1900.

Shenrock, Reverend Joseph C. *Upon This Rock*. Trenton: Diocese of Trenton, 1993.

Smith, Muriel. *From the Hearths of Highlands*. Unpublished.

Smith, Samuel Steele. *Sandy Hook and the Land of the Navesink*. Monmouth Beach: Philip Freneau Press, 1963.

———. *Battle of Monmouth*. Monmouth Beach: Philip Freneau Press, 1963.

Stephens, Jim, ed. *From our Correspondent with the 29th Regiment. Letters from Officers and Men of the 29th New Jersey Volunteers to Monmouth and Ocean County Newspapers, September 1862–June 1863*. Unpublished.

Van Benthuysen, Robert, and Audrey Kent Wilson. *Monmouth County, A Pictorial History*. Norfolk, VA: Donning Co., 1983.

Walsh, Maya. *Joshua Huddy, the Hero Martyr of Monmouth*. Unpublished.

Weiss, Harry B., and Grace M. Weiss *The Early Promotional Literature of New Jersey*. Trenton: New Jersey Agricultural Society, 1964.

"We're Waiting for You, Trudy: Gertrude Ederle Welcome Home Celebration, Parade, Addresses. Tuesday, August 31, 1926 at 3 p.m." Moss Archives.

Wolverton, Chester. *Atlas of Monmouth County, New Jersey*. New York: Chester Wolverton, 1889.

Wroth, Lawrence C. *The Voyages of Giovanni da Verrazzano 1524–1528*. New Haven: Yale University Press, 1970.

INDEX

Noted poet S. Goodenough wrote the following lines celebrating this special community in "the Highlands": "But none have seen such beauteous views / As on the Highlands may be found / The ocean, bay, its wooded heights, / The beach, the shore, the wavelets' roll / Combine to make a picture such / As moves the heart and thrills the soul."